ROKER ROARS BACK

ROKER ROARS BACK

Sunderland's Return to Glory

GEOFF STOREY

MAINSTREAM
PUBLISHING

EDINBURGH AND LONDON

<u>Photo Credit</u>

All the photographs are reproduced by permission of the *Sunderland Echo*.

First published in Great Britain in 1996 by
MAINSTREAM PUBLISHING COMPANY (EDINBURGH) LTD
7 Albany Street
Edinburgh EH1 3UG

ISBN 1 85158 907 4

A catalogue record for this book is available from the British Library

Typeset in Times
Printed and bound in Great Britain by Butler and Tanner Ltd, Frome

CONTENTS

Acknowledgements

I am grateful to my *Sunderland Echo* colleagues and to the following individuals for their help and support in producing this book: John Cairns, Bob Graham, Charles Harrison, Frank Johnson, Bill Mantle, Ian Murtagh and Tim Taylor.

Foreword

Peter Reid

When I got the job I thought Sunderland was a massive football club and, if given the success, the supporters would come to games. I would like to think we are down that road now. We have had a great year for everyone involved in the club and everyone involved with the city. It is their football club. The players have given the city back its pride. The football club reflects the city and I certainly found the people very warm. A lot of industry has gone out of the city and obviously new industries are coming in and things change. But you hope the football club can progress with the city, and now we are up there with the élite it is up to us to stay there. Promotion is a great reflection of the support we've received and moving into a new stadium is going to be important for the club, and the good thing is that it is being built in the heart of the city which is not happening at many football clubs at the moment. It's on the banks of the river on the site of an old colliery so it ties up the old with the new. At the end of the day we have come great strides and it's all credit to the players. Obviously it is up to us to keep the momentum going, which we will try to do.

I wish the book every success and hope it goes well.

1

A Fight for Survival

No club has a divine right to be a member of football's élite, but the big guns of the Premiership will have the welcome mat out for Sunderland for the 1996/97 season. A club deeply steeped in tradition, even dubbed the 'Bank of England' in the 1950s when gates of 60,000 were the order of the day, one of the few remaining 'sleeping giants' is on the march again.

First left behind by Kevin Keegan's revolution at Newcastle then Bryan Robson's instant success in management at Middlesbrough, followers of the once proud Roker Park club found its demise a bitter pill to swallow. Their two north-east rivals are also streets ahead in terms of facilities with St James's Park updated to a magnificent 36,000 capacity all-seater stadium and Middlesbrough celebrating promotion a year ago with a move to the new Riverside ground, bursting at the seams from day one. For the second successive season the Boro have posted 'sold out' signs to potential season-ticket holders. Newcastle, too, had problems accommodating fans desperate for a slice of the action with a season in Europe followed by the Magpies at one stage leading Manchester United by a staggering 12 points in pursuit of a first Championship win for 69 years.

But, thanks to Peter Reid, the catching up is now firmly underway, and for the first time in 20 years the north-east's big three are back in the big time with derby clashes eagerly awaited. Reid, cruelly shown the exit door by Manchester City after finishes in the Premiership of fifth, fifth and ninth, was on soccer's management scrapheap when the Roker board of directors sent out an SOS for his services. Sunderland had slumped to a fourth successive defeat at a wind-swept Barnsley on a bitterly cold Friday night in April 1995 and were again plummeting headlong towards the relegation trapdoor. Swift action was needed if a return to the old Third Division for a second time in less than ten years was to be avoided. Manager Mick Buxton had indicated to the directors that he would leave the club at the end of the season and tentative steps had already been taken to find his successor. Bob Murray, no longer chairman but still very much in control of the purse strings, contacted a Manchester-based journalist to ask after the possible availability of Reid. Vice-chairman Graham Wood explained:

> When I came back from America two weeks ago, I had a meeting with Mick and he intimated to me that, at the end of the season, come what may, his intention was to leave the club. That obviously gave us time to find Mick's successor and, after Monday's board meeting, we assembled at the home of one of the directors to discuss the manager's position.
>
> What we decided was, provided we could get our first choice, we would accelerate the process rather than wait until the end of the season. I met Peter on Tuesday and we reached a two-stage agreement. One for the remainder of the season and the other to be reviewed after that. I phoned Mick on Wednesday morning and asked if I could see him. He asked what it was about and when I said I would rather talk to him he realised what was happening. Mick has Sunderland very much at heart, but how many times have players responded to a new appointment? We were past the transfer deadline so there was nothing more we could do on the playing side. The only thing we could do was on the managerial side and history has proved that often does the trick. We have got a manager of quality and the man we want after a lot of careful consideration. I am very pleased that we have got our number one choice – and that's not always possible.

Reid's brief was no more than survival. He had seven games in a very short space of time to scrap his way out of the bottom three. And he was under no illusions as to the size of the task ahead. 'This is a big club with tremendous potential and I am sure the supporters can play a big part in helping to keep us up,' said the craggy scouser. 'It's obvious they have problems at home where they have won only three games all season. Without wanting to seem big-headed, I have had offers from other clubs to return to management but I was waiting for a club as big as this. This is a massive club with massive potential and we must all do what we can to make sure we are in the First Division next season. I am looking no further than that.'

Two days into the job and on the eve of his first game in charge, the new manager had to face up to the prospect of having points deducted for playing an ineligible player in Buxton's last match. The registration of Dominic Matteo, signed on loan from Liverpool, had not been registered with the Football League before the transfer deadline. 'I had Howard Kendall on the phone and he said I must be the only manager who has played none but lost one,' retorted a bewildered Reid. The punishment administered by the Football League after a 20-minute hearing, however, was a mere rap on the knuckles. The club was fined £2,500 and the England Under-21 international was ordered to return to Anfield.

The next afternoon the players responded magnificently to give Reid the winning start he so desperately needed to instil badly needed confidence into his new charges. He called for patience and was rewarded with an 89th-minute winner from super-sub Craig Russell against Dave Bassett's Sheffield United. 'The team have shown me what they are capable of by beating a team, deservedly so, trying to get promotion,' said Reid. 'But we are not out of the woods yet. We've got six games and they will all be like Cup-ties.' A week later the action switched to the Baseball Ground where Derby County, another side harbouring ambitions of reaching the play-offs, were unable to prevent Reid from chalking up a second successive victory, thanks to Kevin Ball's 41st-minute strike.

'We scrapped and possibly shaded it against a club which, form-wise, is currently the best in the League,' he said. 'Two wins and two clean sheets, which is pleasing. Derby failed to create any clear-cut chances and they have been scoring a lot of goals recently. We are not there yet, but we are getting there. I keep saying I don't set targets because if you do, you can put yourself under pressure with a couple of bad results.'

The maximum six-point haul failed to improve the precarious position, and when mid-table Luton Town forced a 1–1 draw at Roker Park, the safety cushion was five points with four games remaining. And the pressure was back on two days later when Reid made a sentimental return to his beloved Bolton Wanderers. With just five minutes left a deserved goalless draw against a side in second place and firmly on course for the Premiership was in the bag when John McGinlay broke not only the deadlock, but also the hearts of the Roker fans. Reid commented: 'The lads did ever so well and I am sick for them. I've told them that if they keep that attitude up and work like that, we will stay in this division. Bolton are a good side but in the end we got done on a dead-ball which is very disappointing. But that happens in football and it's a lesson that you must concentrate for 90 minutes.'

The big countdown gathered momentum with the visit of Swindon Town, of utmost importance to both clubs. Martin Smith virtually guaranteed survival on his return to the side with the all-important goal and virtually condemned Swindon to the Second Division. 'Beating Swindon was a massive result for us,' said Reid. 'Maybe it's the way I am made, but I want us to be cast-iron certainties.' The facts before the match were simple: Burnley and Bristol City joined Notts County in the Second Division after losing to Portsmouth and Watford respectively and they would be joined by either Sunderland or Swindon. Sunderland needed one win from two matches to be mathematically certain to preserve their status; Swindon had to win all three games. Sunderland had the backing of 6,000 fervent supporters at Turf Moor, and though Smith's early goal was cancelled out the point and Swindon's 3–0 home defeat by Portsmouth meant Reid had achieved his safety target with a game to spare. 'When I took the job on and looked at the fixtures, I thought it was a very difficult job to stay up,' reflected Reid. 'I don't think Sunderland should be in this position and hopefully this is the start to put things right. We are in the First Division, which was the main objective. Now we can go on from here. The support has been magnificent. We can't buy support like that and I am just delighted for everybody at the club. The support at Burnley was just like a home game and that's the biggest compliment I can pay.'

Chairman John Featherstone expressed the gratitude of a board unable to bring in new investment despite advertisements in the Press including the *Financial Times*. 'I have always said management is about motivation and Peter Reid knows how to do that,' said the chairman. 'He is very straight – he and I talk the same language. We should never have been in this position and I can't express how relieved we all are that we have stayed up.'

Mission accomplished, there was just no way Reid wanted to walk away from the next stage of a massive rebuilding programme. Personal terms were not a problem. The stumbling block to signing a two-year contract was the provision of assurances that cash would be spent to strengthen the team. Majority shareholder Murray has been bitterly criticised throughout his ten-year stewardship of the club for not investing more of his personal wealth in the club. He admits manager Denis Smith was greatly underfunded when the club, having lost to Swindon Town in the Wembley play-offs in 1990, took the place of the Wiltshire club in the top flight. Swindon were found guilty of irregular payments, and while third-from-bottom club Sheffield Wednesday contested they should not be relegated, the Football League ruled in Sunderland's favour. The decision not to back Smith with substantial funds totally backfired, and after just one uneventful season, the club was duly relegated and a fortuitous opportunity squandered.

New director John Fickling, however, is on the same wavelength as the supporters and pledged his support and the full backing of the directors.

> All the board, and me in particular, believe we have got to get this club in the Premiership next season. To achieve our aim of the Premiership, we have to give the manager both the resources and the support. That is fundamental. We have to make sure that money is available and that we can satisfy his demands. There is more than one way to give him resources and it's not all about mega bucks. But that does not mean an open-ended cheque-book. It would be an everlasting indictment on this board though if Peter Reid walked out because of our lack of ambition. That does not mean he is judge, jury and executioner. The alternative is to drift along like we have been doing. The only nail-biting I want next year is at the top end of the table.

Reid had a mixture of youth and experience, and on the strength of what he had achieved in seven games at the end of the season, he asked for a minimum £1 million budget. 'He wasn't holding a gun to our head because we were determined to give him what he wanted,' said John Fickling. 'But it wasn't easy. The financial situation was difficult and the directors wanted to ensure funds were made available. There were a lot of meetings between ourselves, and a few sleepless nights on my part, before we could say unequivocally the cash was there.' Most managers want their own backroom staff and Reid was no different, with only youth team coach Ricky Sbragia surviving the clear-out. 'No disrespect to the staff who were already there, but I wanted my own people around me,' he said. 'If you are to be successful, you need to be working with people you are comfortable with.' First-team coach Trevor Hartley and reserve team coach Ian Ross also quickly departed, but there were no hard feelings from the former:

I applaud the foresight of the board and the appointment of Peter Reid, irrespective of what happens to me in the future. There's no doubt that Peter has been the inspiration, even if a few people on the staff have helped out. Managers take the can and I can honestly say he wants the same as Mick Buxton but has gone about it in a totally different way. He has always been a winner and I think not only has he got a personality which the players will accept, he will get on well with the fans. I can't say categorically that we would have gone down, but the position would have been very hard to retrieve. It would have been a hammer blow if we had gone down.

Personally, I believe Peter has got to be given more scope than any previous Sunderland manager. There is enough pressure from within the club with the success of Newcastle and Middlesbrough. Although you say well done to them, you want to be up there as well. Hopefully, under Peter Reid, this club will follow a similar route in a short space of time.

Reid had talks with major shareholder Murray and vice-chairman Graham Wood, and two weeks after another turbulent season had finished he agreed to a new two-year deal. He accepted no substantial funds would be forthcoming: 'I don't think any manager except

Kenny Dalglish at Blackburn Rovers is happy with the amount he's been given to spend. It is very hard to say at the moment just how many changes are needed to make the team competitive. Obviously if somebody comes in with a big offer, I'll have to change my plans. But if you look at where the team finished, then I have a very hard job on my hands. But I feel very comfortable here and I think in a very real sense we've turned the corner.'

The guessing game had already started on the possible comings and goings, but Reid was ahead of the pack. His first move was to prove to be a masterstroke: he appointed former Everton colleague Paul Bracewell assistant manager. Bracewell first joined the Roker ranks in 1984 but lasted only one season before being moved on by Len Ashurst without profit on the initial £250,000 outlay. He returned to Roker Park for a second spell, manager Malcolm Crosby also believing £250,000 was a reasonable fee for a player of Bracewell's calibre. His stay on Wearside this time round may have been much longer, but the circumstances of his leaving were again shrouded with disappointment. Sunderland, again a struggling Second Division team, had defied the odds to reach the 1992 FA Cup Final. There was to be no repeat of the memorable 1973 win over Leeds United, with Liverpool comfortable 2–0 winners at Wembley. Bracewell was out of contract and made it known generally that he would have stayed if offered a new two-year deal. The board, however, were reluctant to meet his demands and Newcastle nipped in to lure him to Tyneside with an independent tribunal also placing a £250,000 valuation on his head. And how well he served Kevin Keegan, helping Newcastle back into the Premier League and playing his part in the Magpies more than consolidating their return to the big time. And even though Sir John Hall was ploughing millions of pounds into the black and whites for Keegan to compete for the best in the transfer market, there was still a part for Bracewell to play.

He had no hesitation, however, of accepting a first challenge in management and linking up again with Reid. Newcastle accepted a nominal fee for the 32-year-old, the £50,000 payment the best piece of business Sunderland had conducted for many a year. 'Appointing Brace was a masterstroke,' said former Everton manager Howard Kendall, now shaping the future of Sheffield United. 'Paul is doing for Peter what Peter did for me, leading by example on the pitch, inspiring team-mates and making sure everyone knows what they are doing. He is a terrific professional, and from what I have seen he has still got what it takes.' Bracewell had no doubts he could handle his added responsibilities and relished a crack on the other side of the fence:

> This is a big challenge for me. It's no secret that I want to break in to the coaching side of the game and I am delighted that everything happened so quickly. I am grateful to Newcastle manager Kevin Keegan and chairman Sir John Hall for agreeing to the move. I still had a year of my contract left with Newcastle, but after three successful years there I am delighted to be here and hope I am as successful in management as I have been as a player. Hopefully this is a step in the right direction for the club. The gaffer and myself have signed two-year contracts on the same day and I hope the supporters are pleased that two players with a lot of Premiership experience have committed themselves to the club.

Reid was delighted to have his former Goodison Park colleague aboard, even though the appointment came as a bit of a surprise considering past events. 'I am not interested in the past,' he said. 'Let's be positive. Paul is a good organiser on the pitch and I am happy with anything that makes my job easier. He is my first signing and that's very important. The fans look to see what type of player you are trying to bring to the club. It's what happens on the pitch and I know this is a step in the right direction. We had three or four good years together at Everton and we are looking to bring that same success to Sunderland. I played in the Premiership last year at 37. Paul is only 32 and I believe his experience will prove invaluable.'

The changes to the backroom staff were quickly finalised with former Blackburn and York City manager Bobby Saxton taking over as first-team coach, Pop Robson quitting Manchester United's successful youth policy to take charge of the reserves, and former manager Alan Durban returning in the role of chief scout to form a formidable management team. On announcing the addition of Saxton to the staff, Reid said: 'I am delighted to have Bobby on board. I have worked with him at Manchester City and I know him from his Blackburn days. He did a terrific job there and he is a good lad.'

Saxton, assistant to Ossie Ardiles at Newcastle four years previously, was assistant manager to Sam Ellis at Blackpool before returning to the north-east. On Durban joining the staff, Reid said: 'I know Alan very well. He has proved himself at Sunderland and has a vast knowledge of the game. He is someone of great experience whose judgement I would back.' Robson, a prolific goalscorer for Newcastle United, with two spells at West Ham and three at Sunderland, was thrilled to be back at Roker. 'I'm delighted to be back, working for Peter Reid,' he said. 'He's a manager full of enthusiasm and he plays football the way I want to. I know Bobby Saxton well too, and I've known Paul Bracewell since his first spell at Roker Park, when I coached under Alan Durban. It's a good team to be working with, and I'm hopeful of a bright future for the club.' Robson played a major role behind the scenes at Old Trafford, an experience he was confident he could put to good use back on Wearside. 'I had four good years at Old Trafford, working with the Director of Youth, Eric Harrison. I've learnt a lot, and I'm happy to have the chance of working here again. There's a special feeling for Sunderland. I was born here and had some good times as a player.'

Before Reid could swing his transfer plans into action, he had to await a decision on the club's request for a further extension to the all-seater deadline. If standing on the Roker terraces was kicked into touch, the club was faced with a ground capacity potentially slashed from 22,000 to under 14,000, even allowing for the installation of 6,000 temporary seats. Plans had been submitted for a 34,000 all-seater stadium on a former pit site at Wearmouth Colliery with a view to completion for the start of the 1997/98 season.

The club's destiny was in the hands of the Football Licensing Authority with chairman John Featherstone warning of the consequences: 'We have had to budget next season on crowds of 14,000,' he said. 'If the FLA gives us another dispensation and we can attract crowds of 22,000, then there will be money to spare. The play-offs have to be our minimum aim but it is paramount we give the manager as much money as possible for new players. We have done our outline budget and we have talked things through with the manager.' Officials were able to breathe a huge sigh of relief when National Heritage Secretary Stephen Dorrell announced an extension for the new season. He said he had granted Sunderland an extension because the club's circumstances were 'sufficiently exceptional'.

Things were going well. Lee Howey accepted a new 12-month deal but Richard Ord came out of contract talks on the eve of the players reporting back for pre-season training with the offer of a two-year contract and testimonial. But before the first training session, a stunned Jimmy Montgomery was sacked from his position as the club's Director of Youth. Hero of the epic FA Cup Final win over Leeds United in 1973 after his double save from Trevor Cherry and Peter Lorimer, the 51-year-old who made a record-breaking 537 League appearances, was staggered by his dismissal.

> It was a bombshell. I had no idea this was going to happen. I can't understand why the manager has waited until now to tell me. It would have been bad enough if he had said something when Trevor Hartley and Ian Ross went.
>
> At least it would have given me more time to try and get fixed up with another job. I've been working 14 hours a day here for the last two years and I am devastated that they can do this to me. Both George Herd (youth team coach) and myself said it would take six or seven years to get the club back on its feet at the bottom end and I would like to think that we have some good lads coming through the Centres of Excellence.

The club had honoured Monty a few years before by naming a new function room at Roker Park the 'Jimmy Montgomery Suite.'

The backroom changes finally completed, Reid switched his attentions to strengthening the squad for the coming season.

As part of Sunderland's preparations, a mini-tour to Ireland included matches against St Patrick's Athletic, Drogheda United and Athlone Town. Peter Reid explained: 'When I was at Manchester City, I always looked forward to the pre-season trip to Ireland. They are competitive matches played in a great environment and the people over there are so friendly. I don't believe pre-season should be torture for the players. I want them to enjoy it and be able to get the best of both worlds.' But squad preparations made slow progress with the work permit application for American international goalkeeper Brad Friedel hitting snags and Burnley refusing to name a price for out-of-contract striker John Mullin.

Sunderland signed the 19-year-old forward subject to a satisfactory independent tribunal fee, but he was among the absentees when the squad headed for Manchester airport. Speculation over Chris Waddle joining the Roker ranks had also gathered momentum throughout the close season, and while waiting to board the aircraft for the short trip across the Irish Sea, Reid finally broke his silence on one of his top targets: 'I made an inquiry for Chris Waddle and I believe that inquiry is ongoing. Sheffield Wednesday manager David Pleat asked for £1 million and I told him that was not realistic at this moment in time. I am just as anxious as anybody to get new people in but as a manager I have learned patience is a quality. Any deal has got to be right for the club. There is not much happening in our division at the moment and when it does, I think it will be like a merry-go-round.'

The six-day break lived up to expectations with the bonus for the Roker camp the discovery of Athlone Town striker Stephen Grant. The 19-year-old denied Sunderland a 100 per cent record by scoring in a 1–1 draw after St Patrick's Athletic had been beaten 2-0 and Drogheda United thrashed 6–0.

Grant, also wanted by Millwall, accepted the offer of a two-year deal in the hope of following in the footsteps of Liam Brady and Roy Keane. The pre-season was completed with away victories over York City, Darlington and Blackpool to raise hopes of an impressive start to the new campaign.

2

A Roker Park Résumé

Few, if any, Sunderland supporters expected to be hailing another Messiah after the immortal Bob Stokoe proudly lifted the FA Cup in 1973. But Peter Reid has joined 'Miracle Bob' as a saviour of a club dying on its feet and in danger of being buried in football's wilderness for years to come.

Surprisingly never voted Manager of the Month, Peter Reid went one better by becoming the first person outside the top flight to be named Manager of the Year by the Football Managers' Association. Not even Alex Ferguson's historic double of leading Manchester United to the Premiership title and an FA Cup Final triumph over Liverpool at Wembley could deny Peter Reid the top accolade awarded by his fellow professionals.

A delighted Peter Reid said: 'It's not often you run out ahead of somebody like Alex and I am truly honoured. I believe the reward is a reflection on the whole of the club.'

Bob Stokoe, and now Peter Reid, restored pride and passion when morale was at such a low ebb; there will always be a place in the hearts of grateful supporters for years to come. Sunderland were a struggling Second Division club just a few months before Stokoe's young braves upset the odds and denied the mighty Leeds United a rare League and Cup double. The season started with high hopes of promotion, but relegation was a more realistic option after four wins in 14 games.

On 1 November 1972 Alan Brown left the club for a second time and four weeks later Stokoe resigned his position as manager of Blackpool to begin an amazing love affair with Wearside. Of the next 23 games, 13 were won and five drawn to propel the club into sixth position. And it was the upturn in form and self-belief which was to make Sunderland such dangerous opponents in the one-off Cup clashes.

But two attempts were needed to dispose of Notts County in the third round, and a home tie against Reading, even with former Roker idol Charlie Hurley at the helm, was not expected to prove too difficult a hurdle to overcome. Sunderland, however, again needed a second bite of the cherry to reach the fifth round and land a mouth-watering tie against the Cup favourites Manchester City.

Goals from Micky Horswill and Billy Hughes, however, silenced the 54,478 Maine Road crowd and the game finished 2–2. The replay at Roker the following Wednesday is still considered one of the greatest nights in the club's history.

Hughes was twice on target but supporters to this day recall a Vic Halom blockbuster which set up a 3–1 win. Again the supporters turned out in their droves, 53,151 witnessing goals from Dave Watson and left-back Ron Guthrie shoot the club into the semi-finals at the expense of Luton Town for the first time since 1956.

Arsenal, bidding for a third successive Wembley triumph, were red-hot favourites to deny the Rokermen their first appearance at the Twin Towers since their only previous win in 1937. But Hillsborough was again to prove a happy hunting ground and when Vic Halom took advantage of a dreadful defensive mix-up, Sunderland were on their way. Billy Hughes added a second goal, and though Charlie George pulled a goal back to set up a nerve-racking finish, the Wembley dream was fulfilled.

Sunderland were the first side from the Second Division for nine years to reach Wembley but there was still more glory to come. To say they were the underdogs is an understatement, but outside Leeds they had fanatical support which helped them upset the odds.

Even when the unlikely right boot of Ian Porterfield fired them into a 31st-minute lead, few expected them to hang on for another hour. But aided by a fantastic double save from goalkeeper Jimmy Montgomery, Sunderland became the first club outside the First

Division in 42 years to win the FA Cup. At the final whistle Stokoe, trilby hat and all, raced across the hallowed Wembley turf to embrace Montgomery. The famous home of English football had not previously seen such delight, but then there had not been many more fairy-tale endings to prompt such amazing scenes.

It was estimated half a million people lined the ten-mile route for the homecoming, many waiting several hours for just a glimpse of their heroes. The loyal fans had good cause to celebrate after several false dawns since relegation from the First Division for the first time in 1958.

A Scottish schoolmaster named James Allen, working at Hendon Boarding School, took the initiative in the foundation of Sunderland in 1879 when they were formed as the Sunderland and District Teachers' Association Football Club at a meeting in the Adults School, Norfolk Street. Because of financial difficulties, they quickly allowed in members from outside the teaching profession, and so became Sunderland AFC in October 1880.

The first captain was Robert Singleton; James Allen became the vice-captain and W. Elliott the secretary. About 20 enthusiasts gathered round the little band and they constituted the committee. In those days the travelling expenses were paid by the players themselves, as well as other incidentals, or by those who were more fortunate in possession of the 'circular'. The first ground was where they encountered such clubs as Sedgefield, Bishop Auckland, Ferryhill, Ovingham, Tyne and Newcastle Rangers.

The club, however, received little support from the public, a county trial match in 1880, for instance, only drawing 6s 2 ½d. At the end of a couple of seasons the club was perilously near dying for want of support. The rent of the field, etc., had been paid by some of the more enthusiastic members, but this could not go on for ever, and when the two seasons had expired the question of disbanding or extending the membership qualification was discussed, and the latter course was decided upon.

In 1881/82 the club moved to a field near the Cedars, but did not remain long there. Before the season was over they were found to be located on a pitch which is now part of the Ashbrooke cricket ground. In that season the club gradually made a name for itself, and reached the semi-final of a trophy competition for clubs in Durham and Northumberland, losing 2–0 to Tyne.

They were still at Ashbrooke in 1882/83 and in that season reached the final, but again failed to win the trophy. This was Sunderland's last season on the south side of the river, for in 1883/84 they pitched up on a piece of ground at the back of the bottom end of Roker Avenue and here the club began to get a hold of the people, although goodness knows they were poor enough for a long time afterwards.

About that time (1883) the Durham Football Association was formed, with Mr Allen – still as enthusiastic as ever – its first secretary, and the Durham County Cup came into existence shortly afterwards. At the close of the 1883/84 season the club made a further move by renting Abbs's Field, Fulwell, not far from the now-defunct tram terminus. In that same season Sunderland made their debut in the English Cup and were knocked out at Redcar in the opening round, and an exact fate befell them in the following season.

It was in this season that Sunderland played their first game in Scotland, paying a visit to Heart of Midlothian in Edinburgh. About a month from the end of the season, the Newcastle Road ground was secured, and what a famous enclosure it became before the club left it!

In the whole history of football there was probably no club that was so hard to beat at home as Sunderland when they occupied that field. In 1887 Robert Thompson became president, James Marr was elected chairman and Samuel Tyzack was the treasurer. To those three gentlemen Sunderland owe much in the football sense, for it was due to their energy and enterprise that the club made its first start in a big way.

They imported some fine players from over the border, and in 1887/88 the team was mostly composed of the pick of Scotland's footballers. Sunderland's last match at the Newcastle Road ground was on 23 April 1898 when they defeated Nottingham Forest 4–0. The next move was to Roker Park, and on 10 September 1898 the opening ceremony was performed by the Marquis of Londonderry in the presence of an estimated 30,000 crowd – the largest 'gate' that had ever assembled on a football ground in the district up to that period.

The fixture that day was with Liverpool for League points, Sunderland winning by the only goal. The club, having made a name for itself, applied to be admitted to the Football League for the 1890/91 season. Their cause was expounded by Mr J.P. Hartley, of Accrington, with such success that they gained admission.

One of the conditions of their election was that owing to their great distance from the majority of clubs they had to pay the travelling expenses of visiting teams. This, however, only continued for the first season, as the Wearsiders, by finishing seventh in the table, had justified their inclusion in that body. Their first league match was at the Newcastle Road ground on 13 September 1890 when they lost 3–2 to Burnley. Two days later they were again beaten at home 4–3 by Wolverhampton Wanderers, after leading 3–0 at the interval. After such a bad start it is pleasing to note that they were not defeated again at home until 9 December 1893 (Blackburn Rovers, 3–2).

From their election to the Football League in 1890, Sunderland enjoyed unbroken membership for 68 years with Arsenal the only club never to have played outside the top flight. During this period six championships were won and on only 16 occasions had the club failed to finish in the top ten. But after relegation for the first time in 1958, they were soon to discover that regaining First Division status is no easy matter, the first season 1958/59 ending in a disappointing 15th position. The 1959/60 season was even worse, but a year later victories over Arsenal, Liverpool and Norwich City in the FA Cup brought mighty Tottenham Hotspur to Roker for a sixth-round tie.

A packed Roker Park crowd of 61,326 witnessed a stirring fight back with Willie McPheat cancelling out a ninth-minute goal from Cliff Jones. In the White Hart Lane replay, however, Spurs delighted a crowd of 64,797 to run out convincing 5–0 winners.

Sunderland, known as the Bank of England club in the 1950s, could not consider themselves short-changed when they paid Middlesbrough £30,000 for a modest young centre-forward, Brian Clough, before the start of the 1961/62 season. Clough didn't disappoint. He scored 29 goals in his first season, including four hat-tricks.

Promotion hopes were at fever pitch when Sunderland travelled to Swansea for the last game of the season needing victory to end a run of four seasons in the Second Division wilderness. But it was not to be, the Swans hanging on for a draw, to the disappointment of the Roker fans who had made the 650-mile round trip.

Clough continued where he had left off and his tally of goals for the 1962/63 season had reached 24 when he was hurt in a collision with Bury goalkeeper Chris Harker, which effectively ended his career. He scored 63 goals in 74 appearances, and though he was to play another three games in the First Division, Sunderland had lost one of the greatest goalscorers of all time.

They only needed a draw from the final game of the season, at home to promotion rivals Chelsea. For the second time, however, they were pipped at the post, Tommy Hamer's first-half goal settling the issue to give his side promotion on goal average.

Sunderland also reached the two-leg semi-final of the Football League Cup, a 3–1 defeat at home leaving them with a mountain to climb in the return at Villa Park, which ended goalless.

There was no slip-up, though, in the 1963/64 season in the chase for the big prize – with only six games lost on the way to finishing in second place behind Leeds United.

Manchester United were given an almighty fright on their way to winning the FA Cup that year. Sunderland were leading 3–1 at Old Trafford with just four minutes left of the sixth-round tie. Bobby Charlton pulled a goal back, and after Jimmy Montgomery had received treatment for a head injury, George Best equalised.

Pre-match scenes for the replay the following Wednesday night were unbelievable, with all roads leading to the ground blocked with thousands of fans determined not to miss out. The official attendance was recorded as 46,727, but a double door at one corner of the ground collapsed and thousands streamed in without paying to swell the gate to an estimated 70,000 with several thousand more locked out.

Sunderland again took the lead through Nick Sharkey, a diminutive striker who shares the club record of five goals in a game with Bobby Gurney. Denis Law grabbed the equaliser, but when Maurice Setters put through his own net in extra-time, Sunderland were back in the driving seat.

Bobby Charlton rescued the Reds two minutes from time to send a pulsating tie into a third meeting at Huddersfield. Sharkey again put Sunderland ahead on the night, but United turned on a scintillating second-half performance to run out 5–1 winners.

The pride was back in Sunderland, though, with the return to the club's rightful place in the First Division the talk of the town. But the club was rocked before a ball was kicked by the decision of Alan Brown to quit and take over at Sheffield Wednesday.

Another blow was the loss of Montgomery through a pre-season injury, leaving Derek Forster to make his debut, at the time the youngest ever goalkeeper and the second youngest player to appear in the First Division at the tender age of 15 years and 185 days. The club remained managerless until mid-November when former England full-back George Hardwick was appointed. He managed to steer the club away from relegation; his reward was to be replaced before the start of the 1965/66 season by Ian McColl.

The Scot fared no better, finishing 19th and only three points clear of relegation. A year later they improved to 15th with no signs of making any impression on the return to the top flight.

McColl was dismissed and the return of the 'Bomber' (Alan Brown) led to a parting of the ways for several senior players and the introduction again of home-grown talent. The release of Charlie Hurley, later to be voted by the supporters as the club's Player of the Century, did the club no favours.

Sunderland's return to the First Division had lasted a mere six seasons, Sheffield Wednesday again slipping through the relegation trapdoor with them in 1970.

Immediately after the end of the 1969/70 season, Sunderland had their first taste of European competition when they were invited to enter the Anglo-Italian competition. The home games yielded a 3–1 win over Lazio and a 2–2 draw with Fiorentina, but defeat in both return games in Italy, 2–1 and 3–0 respectively, ended any further interest in the tournament. Before the start of the 1971/72 season, Sunderland were again invited to compete in the Anglo-Italian Cup. They had to travel to Italy for the first two games, losing 3–2 to Atlanta and beating Cagliari 3–1 to be in with a chance of progressing to the knock-out stages. But home draws in the return again ended interest at the group stage.

The return to the Second Division in the 1969/70 season, for the second time in 12 years was another blow for supporters brought up on life in the top flight, and a season of ups and downs brought a final position of 13th, defeat by Fourth Division Lincoln City in the League Cup and a 3–0 defeat by Orient in the FA Cup.

There was an improvement in the final League table: they finished fifth, but again made early exits from the Cup competitions at the hands of Bristol Rovers (Football League Cup) and Cardiff City in the FA Cup after a third-round win over Sheffield Wednesday. Jimmy Hamilton, making his debut on 29 September 1971 in a 4–1 derby win over Middlesbrough, became the youngest player at the age of 16 years and 103 days to represent the club.

Sunderland made no fewer than 86 changes in the FA Cup-winning season of 1972/73 and a 3–0 defeat in the first round of the Football League Cup at Stoke City suggested there was to be a fairy-tale ending to the FA Cup. In the 20 days before Wembley, Sunderland played eight games and had produced promotion form since Bob Stokoe took over with a return of 30 points from 22 games.

There was no time for extended celebrations. After a 1–1 draw at Cardiff on the Monday night, they returned to a tumultuous homecoming on the Tuesday, then lined up against promotion-chasing Queen's Park Rangers on the Wednesday. A crowd of more than 43,000 turned out to pay homage, but after Mickey Horswill had been sent off, Bob Stokoe had to make an impassioned plea for the game to continue. Sunderland were soundly beaten 3–0.

Sunderland were unable to improve the following year, finishing sixth to runaway champions Middlesbrough and surrendering the FA Cup at the first hurdle to Carlisle in a home replay. The European Cup Winners' Cup adventure also ended prematurely. A 2–0 win in Budapest was followed by a Denis Tueart penalty winner in the return leg at Roker Park. Sunderland took a slender 2–1 lead to Sporting Lisbon and bowed out 3–2 on aggregate.

The Cup-winning team soon broke up, but Sunderland finished fourth and a year later were back in the First Division and on course for another shock Wembley appearance until beaten by Crystal Palace at home in the quarter-finals.

After a disastrous start to the 1976/77 season, Bob Stokoe, against his better judgement, resigned. Only four points were picked up in the first nine games from four draws and after a 1–0 home defeat by Aston Villa with the club bottom of the table, Stokoe walked away from his beloved club.

A run of nine successive defeats, a club record, and ten games on the trot without a goal, another club record, left them well adrift. But astonishing wins over Middlesbrough (4–0), West Brom (6–1) and

West Ham United (6–0) raised hopes of a miraculous escape. The see-saw struggle went to the death. Sunderland needed to draw at Everton, though even if they lost they were safe if either Coventry City or Bristol City won their encounter at Highfield Road. Sunderland had the backing of 10,000 fanatical fans at Goodison Park, but lost 2–0. The game at Coventry started seven minutes late. Bristol City fought back from a two-goal deficit and looked likely winners when Sunderland's defeat was broadcast over the tannoy system. The effect caused the two teams to play out time and though Sunderland lodged an appeal to the Football League, it fell on deaf ears.

The 1977/78 season started moderately and though results perked up, defeats in the opening rounds of both cup competitions by Middlesbrough and Bristol Rovers, a sixth-placed finish was again disappointing.

Jimmy Adamson quit as manager in the October of the following season to join Leeds United; a succession of big-name managers, including Brian Clough and Peter Taylor, Lawrie McMenemy and Bobby Robson, turned the job down. Coach Dave Merrington also turned his back on the job leaving former player Billy Elliott to take over until the end of the season. The run of 14 away games without defeat that season is a club record.

Sunderland started the 1979/80 season with the brash young management team of Ken Knighton and Frank Clark, and on the strength of a magnificent unbeaten home record the club was back in the First Division again. They needed just a point from FA Cup winners West Ham to go up, but did it in style with a 2–0 win thanks to goals from Kevin Arnott and Stan Cummins.

In an amazing Football League Cup replay at St James's Park, Sunderland finally ousted local rivals Newcastle United 9–8 in a penalty shoot-out after an extra-time replay had failed to produce a winner. Manchester City were overcome after a replay but West Ham ended the run, also after a replay at Upton Park.

A John Hawley hat-trick at Maine Road fired Sunderland into pole position in the First Division, but before the season was out, both Ken Knighton and Frank Clark had been sacked by chairman Tom Cowie. Mick Docherty took over for the last four games, and though he started with a 3–0 home win over Birmingham, the relegation trapdoor again beckoned after defeats at the hands of West Brom and Brighton.

Sunderland travelled to Anfield for the last game of the season facing a daunting prospect: if Norwich won, failure to beat Liverpool would lead to an immediate return to the Second Division. Sunderland rocked mighty Liverpool, the reigning European Champions, thanks to a wonder goal from Stan Cummins.

Alan Durban was appointed manager in mid-June and two months later, on the eve of the 1981/82 season, he swooped to pay St Johnstone a club record fee of £350,000 for Ally McCoist. The golden boy of Scotland scored only twice in a disappointing season of 19th position, and the following season the improvement to 16th was only marginal.

Before the start of the 1982/83 season, McCoist was transferred to Glasgow Rangers for a fee of just £205,000 to help finance the arrival of Paul Bracewell from Stoke City for a fee of £250,000. Mark Proctor was signed from Nottingham Forest and other experienced players brought in included Pop Robson, Frank Worthington and Lee Chapman from Chelsea, Southampton and Arsenal respectively.

Durban became the next management casualty with Len Ashurst quickly installed into the vacant chair after the 2 March sacking. Again the club's destiny was to be decided in the last game of the season, and first-half goals from Lee Chapman and Pop Robson at Leicester City did the trick.

Ashurst experienced an amazing season: he led his team out at Wembley for the final of the Milk Cup (Football League Cup), taking the club down into the Second Division, and was sacked when promised his job was safe! Sunderland lost to Norwich City in the Milk Cup Final, Gordon Chisholm deflecting the ball into his own net for the only goal of the game; Clive Walker missed a penalty. But after the 24 March Wembley defeat, only one of the remaining 12 League games was won and it was back to the Second Division for the fourth time in the club's history.

The arrival of Lawrie McMenemy in the close season was greeted ecstatically with supporters convinced an immediate return to the top flight was a mere formality. Chairman Tom Cowie's pledge to 'move heaven and earth' to install 'Big Mac' as manager was fulfilled on 8 July 1985. McMenemy had quit Southampton five weeks previously and, after concluding a family holiday in Florida, he returned to his native north-east with the promise of a seat in the boardroom to become one of the highest paid managers in the Football League.

Tom Cowie said at the time: 'It is a marvellous day for the club, the town, and the area. I would now appeal to the fans for their support. This is the first lucky break I have had. Lawrie is a handsome man being paid a handsome salary. If our fans support us, we will have the cash to support him. I expect this is the start of something big. We must think big and act big. I now expect us to go from strength to strength with promotion and Europe together our aim.'

McMenemy revealed he had turned down several offers, some from outside of football, but was just as enthusiastic as the chairman:

> Everything is possible if we get stuck into it. I am not on an ego trip, that is long gone, and I am not here to project my image. It is not tragic that Sunderland are in the Second Division, it is a matter of fact. We are not big because we are not in the big league. There is no divine right. All we can offer is ourselves and give 100 per cent and I think if we do that our supporters will forgive us for the odd defeat. How long it will take us to get it right, I don't know as I don't have a crystal ball. In my last season at Southampton we got stuffed on the opening day of the season at Sunderland and a few weeks later we were relegation material. But after a lot of hard work we came through to finish fifth. We came through that test and my message here is let's get cracking, but if we fall by the wayside it will not be due to lack of effort as we will be pulling out that little bit extra.

What should have proved to be one of the brightest eras in the club's history became a nightmare scenario over the next 20 months. The first five games of the 1985/86 campaign were all lost and with not a goal in sight, Sunderland were rooted at the foot of the table. The highest they climbed to was 12th, and only with the help of two successive wins in the final games, was relegation just avoided.

The scenes after the 2–0 win over Stoke City were unbelievable. The crowd insisted on a lap of honour from the team and for McMenemy to take a bow, culminating with the waving of a white handkerchief in mock surrender.

Lessons were not heeded from a disastrous season and though hopes were raised after a 2–0 win over Birmingham which took McMenemy's side to the dizzy heights of fifth place, it was all downhill thereafter. A 2–1 home defeat by Sheffield United proved the final straw for irate fans, and when new chairman Bob Murray finally left Roker Park late on the night of 11 April to find his car damaged, he finally pulled the plug on one of the most miserable managerial appointments in the club's long and distinguished history.

The golden dream was shattered. A glittering career lay in ruins. He had arrived to the enthusiastic roar of fans. He left amid a clamour of bitterness and despair. It was an expensive gamble that failed. He had fallen victim to the pressures of disgruntled fans, backroom bickering and, it had to be faced, inadequate performance. The solutions that succeeded brilliantly at Southampton failed miserably at Roker. Big Mac said he wanted to stay on:

> My pride and instincts told me to stay, but a number of factors have influenced me in the last few days. When I considered them, I decided it was best for me to get out. I am not leaving because the players are not playing for me. But there has been so much adverse publicity surrounding Roker since my arrival two years ago, I genuinely believe if I go it will take the pressure off the players.
>
> In 20 years of management I cannot remember a team so full of fear as the one I put out against Sheffield United last Saturday. We were beaten and I could not be surprised at the result. I desperately want them to stay up – in fact, they must avoid relegation. I feel with me leaving and taking all the controversy about big salaries and boardroom battles with me, they should get the peace and quiet they need to concentrate on football.

Bob Stokoe made a sentimental return to fill the position until the end of the season, with a similar brief to Peter Reid – keep the club up at all costs for the remaining seven matches. He called on the spirit of '73 to escape the dreaded drop.

Stokoe said at the time:

> We have to plough everything into a seven-game and three-week period and that is all I am interested in. It is a completely different

situation to when I came here last time. People go away on holiday for longer. There is [*sic*] no cups to hang our hats on this time – it's just a matter of surviving. Lawrie has resigned and if that's what the fans wanted, then that's what they've got. My future is not important. The future of Sunderland Football Club is at stake and all I am interested in is keeping them in the Second Division. It would be a tragedy if they went down.

My job is to lift the fear out of the dressing room and get a bit of confidence back into the players, but that will only come with results. One thing is for sure, there will have to be a lot better return than there has been from the last six matches when only one point was forthcoming.

Stokoe got off to a bad start, losing 3–2 at Bradford City, but a couple of wins and a couple of draws took him to the brink of safety. But astonishingly his side not only squandered a two-goal lead in the last game of the season, but also missed a penalty to condemn Sunderland to the dreaded play-offs against a Gillingham side who had just missed out on automatic promotion from the Third Division.

Tony Cascarino took full advantage of dreadful defending to help Gillingham establish a 3–2 lead from the first leg. In a topsy-turvy return Sunderland were always up against it after again missing a penalty, and though Keith Bertschin scored an extra-time winner, Gillingham won on the away goals rule and Sunderland were relegated to the Third Division for the first time in their proud history.

Plenty of big management names were again in the frame. Bob Murray made an astute move when he turned to another brash up-and-coming York City management team of Denis Smith and Viv Busby to lead the club out of unknown territory. Smith was so confident of his own ability he agreed to pay half of the £20,000 compensation due to his former employees if he failed to win promotion at the first attempt in 1987/88 season.

His first two signings – full-back John Kay from Wimbledon and his former York City skipper and central defender, John McPhail – may not have whet the appetite of the Roker fans, but they were to play a vital part in the task ahead. A second return to his former club to snatch Marco Gabbiadini for a fee of £80,000 proved a snip. Sunderland were in tenth position when the powerful and lightning-fast striker made his debut in a shock 2–0 home defeat by Chester

City. But he was to score 21 crucial league goals, and with seven wins from the last eight games Smith's side clinched the Third Division Championship in style. Promotion was guaranteed in the third from last match at Port Vale, the title two days later against Northampton, and a 4–1 romp at Rotherham brought down the curtain on the club's only season ever in English football's third tier with a record haul of 93 points. A first-hurdle Littlewoods Cup (Football League Cup) defeat by Middlesbrough and exits from the Freight Rover Trophy and FA Cup at the hands of Hartlepool and Scunthorpe failed to dampen the spirits of the Sunderland supporters.

The first season back in Division Two ended with a consolidating position of 11th with Gabbiadini going one better in the goalscoring stakes with a total of 23 League and Cup goals. On 20 September 1989 Paul Bracewell signed on a permanent basis after a successful loan period and the side was hardly ever out of a play-off position throughout the campaign. A 3–2 home defeat by Oldham Athletic in the last match set up the mouth-watering prospect of a two-leg showdown against Newcastle with the prize a Wembley final against Swindon Town. Paul Hardyman was sent off after missing a penalty in the goalless home draw to make Newcastle firm favourites in the return, but goals from Eric Gates and Marco Gabbiadini silenced a 32,199 St James's Park crowd.

Sunderland were completely outplayed by a slick Ossie Ardiles side and had goalkeeper Tony Norman to thank for keeping the scoreline down to a single goal defeat. But Swindon were found guilty of irregular payments and Sunderland were awarded their place in the First Division.

Again a lack of investment proved decisive. Kevin Ball and Peter Davenport were the only pre-season signings and it became obvious throughout the 1990/91 campaign another desperate struggle was in store. Sunderland never got out of the bottom two for the last dozen games and, amid emotional scenes at Maine Road, they forfeited their place in the top flight again. Sunderland were thrashed 6–0 in the League Cup at Derby County and crashed out of the FA Cup 4–1 to Everton.

Just nine games into the 1991/92 season, Marco Gabbiadini was transferred to Crystal Palace for a record £1.8 million fee, with York City agreeing to £300,000 up front as settlement of a 25 per cent knock-on agreement. He had scored 87 goals in 183 appearances. Denis Smith quickly brought in Anton Rogan and John Byrne, but it was ten weeks before the club paid a record fee of £900,000 for Don Goodman to replace the departed Gabbiadini.

After just four matches, however, Denis Smith was sacked and Malcolm Crosby, who started the season as youth team coach and replaced Viv Busby as senior coach, took over as caretaker manager. Goodman, who played in the first round of the FA Cup for his previous club West Brom, was to miss out on another remarkable Wembley trail. Crosby won his first five games and won the Manager of the Month award in his first month in charge, and though his position in the hot seat remained a constant worry, after victories over First Division clubs West Ham and Chelsea (both went to a replay), Sunderland beat Norwich City in the semi-final at Hillsborough. John Byrne went into the final against Liverpool chasing a personal milestone, and had he tucked away an early chance, he would have become only the tenth player to score in every round of the competition. Goals from Michael Thomas and Ian Rush set up Liverpool's fifth FA Cup success.

Crosby was always walking a tightrope and though he was given the go-ahead to sign Grimsby Town captain Shaun Cunnington for £650,000 and John Colquhoun from Hearts at a cost of £250,000, John Byrne returned to Brighton and another season of drifting along aimlessly resulted in Crosby being shown the door in bizarre circumstances. The game at Tranmere on 30 January 1993 was postponed, and with the pools panel awarding a home win, he was given the axe on the Monday morning!

Four days later former England international Terry Butcher, given the chance at the start of the season to resurrect his playing career, took over as player-manager. A disaster at Coventry City in his first stint as a manager, the former Ipswich Town and Glasgow Rangers defender fared no better and but for a series of results on the last day of the season which went their way, Sunderland survived another relegation by the skin of their teeth.

Even so, Butcher was given more money than any other manager in the club's history. He brought in Derek Ferguson (Hearts), Andy Melville (Oxford United), Phil Gray (Luton Town) and Ian Rodgerson at a cost of over two million pounds, and goalkeeper Alec

Chamberlain arrived on a free transfer from Luton Town. He made the fatal mistake, however, at the end of the previous season of stating that several players had outstayed their welcome and would not be around at the start of the new campaign.

A car crash involving his new signings ruled Gray and Rodgerson out of the opening game of the 1993/94 season, a 5–0 defeat at Derby County, and it soon became evident all was not well in the camp. On the strength of five successive defeats, Butcher was sacked, but again the way the directors went about their business was unbelievable. Butcher was driving to the ground as usual to arrive at nine o'clock when he heard on his car radio that he was to be replaced as manager. An hour elapsed before he emerged to say that if he had been sacked he must have missed it. Eventually, chairman Bob Murray arrived, Butcher's and his right-hand man Ian Atkins's dismissal was confirmed, chief coach Mick Buxton was appointed manager, and Murray handed in his resignation in the space of a few minutes, leaving behind them all a trail of bewildered sports writers, radio commentators and television crews.

Buxton's organisation averted another crisis and a comfortable mid-table finish raised hopes of a genuine promotion push in the 1994/95 season. Under his guidance the best unbeaten start since the 1910/11 season was made, but only two of the eight games yielded victories.

The old problem of limited transfer funds prompted the sale of Don Goodman to Wolves for a fee of £1.4 million, but instead of bringing in a replacement striker, Buxton finally landed full-back Martin Scott from Bristol City in an exchange deal with Gary Owers. It was not until transfer deadline day that Brett Angell was signed from Everton for a fee of £600,000, but before the newcomer could repay the manager's faith in him, Buxton was relieved of his duties to make way for the arrival of Peter Reid.

3

Reid Kicks Off

The Football League computer did Sunderland no favours with three of their first five fixtures in the 1995/96 season against the clubs relegated from the Premiership. And when Leicester City won by the odd goal in three at Roker Park on the opening day of the season, there was an air of despondency on the terraces. Leicester took just nine minutes to breach the Roker defence, Australian international Steve Corica celebrating his debut with a cracking goal. And though Steve Agnew scored against his former club, Mark Robins restored City's lead to emphasise the class gap between the Premiership and the Endsleigh League. Peter Reid reflected:

> We came up against a well-organised side who got two great strikes and, on the day, we were not good enough to break them down. When you look back over the years, teams come here and make it tight and we run out of patience. I know that and it's something me as manager and the coaching staff have got to do something about.
>
> It's not the end of the world. There's money available and I have been trying to do things. I know what I want and in the end I think I will get it – hopefully sooner rather than later. I have known from day one that I need to add to the squad, and that's not having a go at the players. But I have to improve the squad and bring new players in.

His hopes of landing American goalkeeper Brad Friedel, however, were dashed by the Department of Employment. The authority informed the club it did not believe Friedel met its criteria in relation to international appearances in competitive matches. 'I was sure the lad met the criteria to obtain a work permit,' said Reid. The club was unsuccessful with an appeal, leaving Alec Chamberlain the only experienced goalkeeper on the books.

The first round of the Coca-Cola Cup presented an interesting challenge against Third Division Preston. Brett Angell, a £600,000 signing from Everton on transfer deadline day, finally broke his goalscoring hoodoo. He had failed to get off the mark and make his presence felt in the battle to avoid relegation and his 50th-minute breakthrough was to prove to be his only contribution throughout a nightmare season. Ryan Kidd, however, ensured the return leg was not a complete formality when he headed an equaliser for the Third Division club.

Before that second leg came a tough trip to Carrow Road, and Sunderland were full value for the first point on the board with Norwich manager Martin O'Neill's prediction proving to be spot on. 'Sunderland will go very close to promotion,' said the former Northern Ireland international. 'They played very well and they are a fine passing team. We could not get the ball. I probably know more about the Endsleigh League than the players and the supporters here. They are used to watching Premiership games here on Sky. I've seen loads of games and this is going to be a very hard division to get out of and, if it was not brought home at Luton in our first match, my word it was by Sunderland.'

Paul Stewart was signed on a month's loan from Liverpool, determined to grab another lifeline with both hands. He said: 'I'm chomping at the bit to play – I want to show I am still the player I was. I am under contract at Liverpool but the writing is on the wall. I'm not in the plans there and all I want is to get a club. I'm looking forward to playing again. I miss the competitive games. I've played a few reserve games but it's not the same.'

Loan spells at Crystal Palace, Wolves and Burnley failed to lead to a permanent deal for the former England international, the £1 million price tag frightening off the trio of interested clubs. 'I've been to too many clubs on loan and been promised too many things,' added

Stewart. 'I know the First Division through my times at Burnley and Wolves and I got a winners' medal with Crystal Palace when they went up.' Stewart was not eligible for the Cup-tie against Preston and Steve Agnew was ruled out for six weeks after travelling to London for an Achilles operation.

The newcomer could have been excused if he had requested his temporary registration to be torn up and he had headed back to Anfield after watching his new colleagues in action for the first time. Preston scored twice before half-time and were on course for one of the shock results of the first round. But they reckoned without the fighting spirit instilled by Reid into his side, and two goals in a minute immediately after the break rescued Sunderland from total embarrassment.

Lee Howey grabbed a late winner and the Sunderland players woke up next morning to learn the remarkable fight-back had been rewarded with a two-leg crack against Coca-Cola Cup holders Liverpool.

But it was back to the bread and butter of a first League win against the pre-season promotion favourites Wolves. And how Reid's side rose to the challenge – with first-half goals from Andy Melville and Phil Gray sending the Wolves packing! A hectic first month to the season was concluded at Port Vale when Sunderland had to overcome the shock of conceding a second-minute goal to extend an unbeaten run to five matches. Phil Gray was again on target when Stewart finally got in on the action as a second-half substitute.

At the end of August with all clubs having played four games, Sunderland were in 14th position and trailed leaders Millwall by five points.

		P	W	D	L	F	A	Pts
1	Millwall	4	3	1	0	5	2	10
2	Barnsley	4	3	0	1	10	8	9
14	Sunderland	4	1	2	1	4	3	5

Hopes of making up the leeway against Ipswich Town, the Premiership's bottom club the previous season, were shattered by an Alex Mathie hat-trick at Portman Road. The former Newcastle United striker fired Ipswich level on points with the leading clubs in an astonishing match. Stewart was given his chance in the starting line-up only to hobble off with a knee injury which was to keep him out of action for six months. Reid is no stranger to racecourses and he couldn't resist a quip on the day's events:

> I don't think I would have backed a winner today. I've been involved in games all through my career where you come out and get turned over and have won. Usually it's a one-niller, rarely is it three. Anyone looking at it will say we were turned over. After the first-half it was ridiculous that we were two down. I thought we were the better team and just didn't finish. The lads had every right to be sick when I went into the dressingroom. But that's football and you have to get goals. We have to dust ourselves down and find a killer instinct. We've played some good stuff, but that's no use to me.

Former Scottish international Derek Ferguson, valued at £650,000 when signed from Hearts two years previously, was transferred to Falkirk in a cut-price £150,000 deal. Shaun Cunnington was also allowed to leave on the cheap to make a fresh start at West Brom. Another midfield player who cost £650,000 when signed from Grimsby Town, he linked up again with former boss Alan Buckley at the Hawthorns. The fee was expected to eventually boost the Roker coffers by £220,000 related to appearances, but injuries will keep the price down to a nominal six-figure sum.

Southend, beaten 8–0 on their first ever visit to Roker Park in the 1987/88 Third Division Championship season, had won on their four subsequent visits and, though struggling at the wrong end of the table, were expected to make it tough. And when skipper Kevin Ball was sent off on the hour for a second bookable offence, another disappointing result looked a possibility. Sunderland were ahead through Craig Russell's first goal of the season and the victory proved to be the start of an unbeaten eleven-match run in the League. 'We did not pass the ball as well as I wanted when we had 11 men, but we got a result from a quality goal,' said Reid. 'We played better at Ipswich and did not get a result, but that's football so you have to take what you can.'

Failure to beat Portsmouth after being in the lead for 80 minutes was another set-back for the Roker Park fans. A goal to the good after just six minutes, Phil Gray had a penalty kick saved, and to add insult to injury, Alan McLoughlin made no mistake from the penalty spot to give the visitors an unexpected point.

A first away win of the season put the smile back on the faces of the travelling supporters who made the long trip to Kenilworth Road for the match against a Luton Town side destined once more to struggle against relegation. John Mullin opened the scoring with his first goal for the club in only his second start, and when Phil Gray increased the lead his former club slumped to a fifth successive defeat. Sunderland could even afford the luxury of a fourth successive penalty miss, Richard Ord joining Martin Scott and Phil Gray (twice) on the list of failures.

The limited cash budget was not burning a hole in Reid's pocket, but he confirmed he had offers on the table for Wolves striker David Kelly and Chris Waddle. Wolves were demanding almost £1 million for Kelly and Reid's valuation for Waddle was only half the £750,000 wanted by Sheffield Wednesday.

'I have made a bid for David Kelly and I intend to speak to Graham Taylor again,' said Reid. 'I made a bid for Chris Waddle and that was also turned down. I won't be held to ransom. Waddle is a class act but at 34 going on 35, you've got to be careful what you pay.' There were to be further talks and speculation linking Waddle with a return to his native north-east, but that's as far as the protracted deal went with Reid finally abandoning his attempts to add the silky skills of the former England winger to his squad.

But he finally brought in the proven goalscorer he had been chasing all summer when Kelly, having played a big part in helping Newcastle into the Premiership, returned to the north-east hot-bed of soccer.

Kelly had rejected Sunderland manager Denis Smith in favour of signing for the Magpies where he won a First Division Championship medal. The deal was only worth £300,000, when Smith had cash to spend from the £1.8 million transfer of Marco Gabbiadini to Crystal Palace.

Kelly scored a hat trick for Newcastle in the final game of the promotion winning season – a 7–1 win over Leicester City – and never played for them again. He scored 28 goals in the promotion season only to be sold to Wolves for £750,000. He was out of favour at Molineux as manager Graham Taylor opted for a strike force of former Sunderland favourite Don Goodman and Steve Bull.

The deal – an initial £900,000 and a further payment of £100,000 if Sunderland clinched promotion – went through too late for the Republic of Ireland international to make his debut in the dream Coca-Cola Cup-tie at Anfield.

Kelly expressed his delight at being back in the area and was confident in his own ability to help fire Sunderland into the Premiership: 'Coming back is very pleasing even if it has all happened so quickly,' he said. 'I am disappointed that the deal was not completed in time to play at Liverpool, but I will be there. I have heard good reports about Peter Reid. Niall Quinn said you get nothing but honesty and that's good enough for me. Wolves accepted a bid for me and if you are not part of the manager's plans, you pack your bags and move on.'

Kelly could only watch in anguish as his new team-mates let Liverpool off the hook in their own back-yard. With the tie evenly balanced on play, Liverpool were ahead thanks to Steve McManaman's eighth-minute rocket, the penalty hoodoo struck again. Goalkeeper David James upended Paul Bracewell and Loughborough referee Peter Jones had little support when he only showed the goalkeeper the yellow card and not red for his misdemeanour. James stayed on and made amends by beating away Michael Gray's spot kick to the delight of his relieved colleagues. Stan Collymore, still struggling to justify his record-breaking £8.5 million move from Nottingham Forest, was replaced by Michael Thomas. The substitute, who opened the scoring when the sides met in the 1992 FA Cup Final at Wembley, had only been in the action for eight minutes when he curled a 25-yarder into the top corner to give the holders a two-goal cushion for the return leg.

Sunderland returned to League action at the New Den and though Kelly made his debut, he declined the opportunity of a 44th-minute penalty to open his goalscoring tally. Martin Scott grabbed the ball after Kelly had been brought down and the left-back confidently beat Kasey Keller. Millwall equalised against the run of play and controversy still raged after the game as to who should be credited with Sunderland's winner. Martin Smith claimed he got the faintest of touches with a glancing header from Mick Gray's free-kick with his colleague adamant the ball flew straight into the net.

'Definitely my goal,' said Gray. 'The free-kick went straight in.' Smith responded: 'The ball flicked off my head. Definitely my goal.' There was no argument as to who was the best team. Sunderland won hands down against one of the early-season promotion pace-setters.

Away draw specialists Reading denied Sunderland a move into second place behind Leicester City. The visitors, beaten in the play-off final at Wembley the previous season, were twice in the lead until Kelly's first goal for the club and Andy Melville's last-gasp equaliser saved the day. Kelly's gut reaction was to claim Sunderland were better equipped than Newcastle to win promotion:

> Let's put it this way – Sunderland are a lot stronger than Newcastle were when I first joined them. It was a real struggle initially and in this side there is a lot of confidence. But it's too early to be talking about the Newcastle side I left. Obviously everything went perfect the year we went up. I would say Sunderland are somewhere in between, but, in my experience, the hard part is to get up there rather than stay there. Once you are up there it tends to lift you. We are now within striking distance and it's a real pleasure to be playing in this team.

The First Division table at the end of September read:

		P	W	D	L	F	A	Pts
1	Leicester City	10	6	2	2	16	11	20
2	Barnsley	10	5	2	3	16	18	17
3	Millwall	9	5	2	2	8	5	17
4	Charlton	10	4	4	2	15	10	16
5	Huddersfield	10	5	1	4	15	14	16
6	Sunderland	10	4	4	2	10	10	16

Within striking distance of the early promotion leaders, a packed Roker Park welcomed mighty Liverpool for the return leg in the Coca-Cola Cup. There was to be no fairy-tale outcome, however, as the dismissal of Martin Smith and England full-back Rob Jones grabbed the headlines. Sunderland were again more than a match for the aristocrats of Anfield until an unsavoury 27th-minute incident robbed Sunderland of their England Under-21 international.

Robbie Fowler put the fans out of their misery early in the second half and closed the door firmly on a possible shock result. Liverpool went through 3–0 on aggregate. 'Losing Smith knocked our shape a bit,' admitted Reid. 'We had worked out a plan and losing him meant that went out of the window. We were playing against a quality side and it shows what we have to achieve. I tried to keep it tight at the back but Robbie Fowler turned us with a brilliant finish. We had our chances and did not put them away. But we are getting there. We played well over the two legs and I just wish we had got a goal.'

Sunderland were caught up in a club v. country wrangle on the eve of the visit to Selhurst Park with Northern Ireland finally relenting to give Phil Gray the go-ahead to play against Crystal Palace. The Irish insisted on invoking the five-day rule preventing players from turning out at club level after previously informing clubs they had no objections. Calm restored, Sunderland at last served notice they were a force to be reckoned with in the promotion chase. They could even afford the luxury of two missed penalties on their way to a third successive victory. Martin Scott hit the post in the first minute and after David Kelly had scored the all-important goal, Paul Bracewell fired wide from the spot. It was Sunderland's seventh miss in eight attempts.

Kelly took stock of the promotion scene before heading off to link up with the Republic of Ireland squad for the European Championship qualifier against Latvia in Dublin:

> It's not the best League I have played in. Over the last few years there have always been teams like Newcastle and Middlesbrough, who have been outstanding. But, at the moment, I can't see anybody pulling clear. I've seen most of the teams who are supposed to be the best, but nobody really catches the eye. In all honesty, it could be one of a dozen teams, so why not us instead of somebody else?

And while Reid continued to keep his feet firmly on the ground, the cock-a-hoop manager said: 'I have not seen a better side in this division than us this season. We have done very well in the first quarter of the programme, but there is still a long, long way to go.

This is a very tight division as bottom club Port Vale proved by winning at Huddersfield. We've got to keep it going and I have always said if we can get consistency, we must have a chance.'

Kelly replaced two-goal hero John Aldridge for the Republic of Ireland only to be stretchered off to leave Reid cursing the luck of the Irish. The manager was in his car listening to commentary on the England v. Norway game when reports were switched to the Republic's match. 'Mark Lawrenson said the Irish were going to make a substitution, bringing John Aldridge off,' said Reid. 'I was saying to myself "You are winning, bring a midfield player on and close the game down." But when he said they were bringing David Kelly on for the last few minutes, I couldn't believe it.' And Watford were in no mood to offer any consolation and boost promotion prospects. The visitors hit back to grab a point after Martin Scott had broken the deadlock with a stunning free-kick. Scott emerged a winner though, backing himself at odds of 22 to 1 to score the first goal to the delight of his father and a couple of team-mates.

Sunderland's next match was the shortest trip of the season to Huddersfield where again they had to settle for a point. Kelly was not fully match-fit and paid the penalty in another stop-go start to his Roker career. He had limped off before Phil Gray struck in the last five minutes, though his fellow striker remained confident the partnership would thrive. 'David Kelly is a prolific goalscorer,' said Gray. 'I am hoping to chip in with my 15 to 20 goals and if David can improve on that, it will be brilliant. He has got a great touch and he is so clever on the ball. I have played with a few different partners since I joined the club but the partnership is just starting to gel. If we keep improving there is no reason why this partnership should not be one of the best in the First Division – we will get goals.'

Unfortunately, the pair were only in action for four more games due to injury and the loss of two experienced international strikers would have proved too much for most sides in the division.

Barry Venison was linked with a return to Roker Park only for Reid to reveal the kitty was bare and any further transfer activity must be self-financed. Quizzed on whether he was interested in ending Venison's nightmare stint in Turkey, he said: 'You had better ask the money man. I would like to strengthen the squad like any other manager in the Football League, but I am the manager and I am skint.' Three directors had had to dip into their own pockets to prop up the £900,000 signing of Kelly, and as attendances had only reached the break-even figure and the overdraft had reached a £1½ million ceiling, cash for players was a non-starter. Chief executive John Fickling moved quickly to stamp out any suggestion of a rift between the directors and manager:

> There is no rift between the board and the manager. Both parties are working towards achieving maximum results for team building and it's crazy to suggest otherwise. Like any other club we have not got unlimited funds but there are one or two businessmen still around who could be interested. Yes, we need more funds, and I would not rule out anything happening. The new ground is moving at pace and when completed will take this club on to another level. Our aim is to get into the Premiership as soon as possible, when our circumstances will be completely different. We would need a lot of money and the new ground is essential. This is the time to be positive.

The promotion challenge was sustained with the help of a hard-earned 2–1 win over Barnsley with goals from Craig Russell and Lee Howey, with Reid full of admiration for the players sticking to the task.

> Since I have been here, we have lost only three of 21 League games. The players are right behind me and the club and are proud to wear the shirt. Their attitude has been first class. I was at a Premier club as a manager for two and a half years and I know what it takes to finish fifth twice and ninth. These players have been superb, from getting into a battle with the last seven games of last season to keep this club in the First Division and, at the same time, trying to play football. I've got nothing but admiration for them. They know it's all down to hard work and that we've got to keep it going. Even in the games we've drawn, we've tried to be positive. If we keep being positive we will come unstuck in a couple of games but, overall, I think we will get results.

The top of the First Division at the end of October read:

	P	W	D	L	F	A	Pts
1 Millwall	14	8	4	2	17	11	28
2 Birmingham	14	7	4	3	24	14	25
3 Leicester City	14	7	4	3	24	18	25
4 West Brom	14	7	3	4	20	15	24
5 Sunderland	14	6	6	2	17	13	24

4

The Run-up to Christmas

Sunderland have always enjoyed a successful youth policy dating back to the 1950s when Alan Brown preferred to bring in home grown talent in preference to experienced internationals. Brown was appointed manager on 1 August 1957, and 10,000 were there for the first practice and 56,493 for the opening game of the season, a 1–0 home defeat by Arsenal. The first eight games brought only four points and when Charlie Hurley's debut in a 7–0 defeat at Blackpool was followed in the next match at Burnley with a six-goal drubbing, the writing was on the wall.

Brown stuck to his convictions over blooding youngsters with the likes of Silksworth Juniors full-back Alan Graham, left-winger John Goodchild from Ludworth Juniors, Alan Spence from Murton Juniors, Jack Maltby (Crookhall Juniors), local lad Alan O'Neill, and Graham Reed from King's Lynn all thrown in at the deep end and asked to do a man's job. Ambrose Fogarty was bought from Glentoran for a fee of £4,500 and won Eire international caps from the right wing; George Whitelaw cost £5,000 when signed from St Johnstone, his five appearances averaging out at a grand apiece; Don Kitchenbrand was brought in from Glasgow Rangers for a fee of £15,000; and Reg Pearce's move from Luton Town cost £16,000.

The slide continued and a 7–1 hammering at Luton was the start of four defeats on the trot to plunge the only club never to have played outside the First Division on the brink.

A 2–2 draw at Old Trafford on the Good Friday raised hopes but a 6–1 home defeat by Birmingham City 24 hours later set the alarm bells ringing loud and clear again. Manchester United won 2–1 at Roker Park on Easter Monday before a crowd of 51,328 and when Manchester City inflicted a 3-1 defeat at Maine Road, relegation was all but unavoidable. Sunderland gave themselves an outside chance by beating Nottingham Forest 3–0, and they travelled to Portsmouth knowing victory at Fratton Park could save them if other results went their way. A Kitchenbrand double gave Sunderland a 2–0 win but sadly it was not enough. Leicester City, who had lost more away games than any other side and had conceded 112 goals, won 1–0 at Birmingham.

Brown was never forgiven by thousands of supporters, who claimed he had been too intent on building a young side when other options were available. His decision to develop a successful youth policy was to pay dividends in the long-term though the club has always struggled to hang on to promising youngsters when tempted with big cash offers. Peter Reid resisted bids for Martin Smith and Craig Russell, and he soon rewarded 18-year-old winger Sam Aiston and exciting 17-year-old striker Michael Bridges with improved and extended contracts. Aiston, rejected by Newcastle when he put education before football, put the Northern Intermediate League firmly behind him and Bridges, still eligible for the youth team for a further two seasons, also bid farewell to his YTS colleague on match-days. Aiston recalled:

> All I was hoping for this year was to win myself a contract by the end of the season. That was the target I set myself. It was quite tough at Newcastle because I was tied up with my A-levels at the same time and Newcastle ended up letting me go. It was Jimmy Montgomery who gave me the chance here, encouraging me to come along and get involved, and it has just gone on from there. In footballing terms, what I was aiming for this season was to establish myself in the reserves. I wasn't expected to be included in the first team and I was very nervous before the games.
>
> My first game wasn't too bad because I was coming on as a substitute and, with me being so young and unknown, there wasn't

any pressure or expectation on me. But when I was playing in the first full game I think the nerves sapped my energy and I was very tired by the end. I'm enjoying the whole thing though. Peter Reid has been a very important influence on my game.

But Reid turned to experienced Newcastle goalkeeper Mike Hooper for his next sortie into the transfer market. Squeezed out at St James's Park by Czech international Pavel Srnicek and the arrival of Shaka Hislop from Reading, the former Liverpool keeper jumped at the chance of a fresh start at Roker. Reid's positive approach of sticking with three outfield players on the substitutes bench gave Hooper no chance to prove himself at senior level. Assistant manager Paul Bracewell said:

We decided at the start of the season to go with three outfield players, though there is always the chance we will get caught out at some stage of the season. Hopefully that won't happen, but we have contingency plans should Alec Chamberlain pick up an injury in a match and I don't see why we should change. It shows we are being positive and when we have brought three substitutes on, we have usually got a result from it. We don't make changes just for the sake of it and, fortunately, we have not been hit by too many injuries. The successful teams are the ones that go through the season with a settled side, using as few players as possible.

Hooper made the trip to the Valley for Sunderland's first appearance before the live television cameras but, as expected, he was no more than a mere spectator in a 1–1 draw. The TV audience witnessed first-hand the goalscoring problems in a seventh draw from 15 matches.

International calls led to the postponement of the visit of Tranmere Rovers with Phil Gray travelling to Austria with Northern Ireland, David Kelly linking up with the Republic of Ireland and Andy Melville with Wales for the trip to Albania for crucial European Championship qualifying group matches. There was an added bonus for the club when Michael Gray was named in the Football League squad to meet the Italian League Serie B at Huddersfield, and Martin Smith was placed on standby.

A phone call, however, from Football League manager Brian Horton led to Smith interrupting his 21st birthday celebrations and joining Gray in the starting line-up. Both passed their first League representative test with flying colours in the 1–1 draw in front of an audience including Liverpool manager Roy Evans, Nottingham Forest's Frank Clark, Aston Villa's Brian Little and David Pleat of Sheffield Wednesday.

'It came as a shock when I got the call on Sunday morning,' said Smith. 'I have been on stand-by before for the England Under-21 squad, but nothing has happened. I expected to be a substitute, but when the manager named the team it was great for me. I enjoyed the game, but it was much more physical than when I came on as a substitute against the Republic of Ireland at St James's Park last season.'

Gray, too, found the tight marking of the Italians alien to what he has experienced. 'It was a great experience, completely different to anything I have ever played in,' he said. 'Sometimes I had three or four players around me and I found it hard to adapt. But it was a tremendous experience for both Martin and myself and hopefully just the start of more to come. We've been away for three days and just training and being with the best young players in the country is an experience. Martin has been away previously, but it was my first time and I have really enjoyed it.'

Brian Horton was impressed: 'I have probably seen more of the two Sunderland players than anybody,' he said. 'I thought they both did very well and though Smith has been out three games through suspension, he is quality.'

Smith had to be content with a place on the substitutes bench for the home game against Sheffield United, replacing Craig Russell in the second-half of a 2–0 win. And it was Phil Gray, fresh from scoring for the Irish in midweek, who blunted the Blades. His double, his first goals at home for three months, hoisted Sunderland into fourth place. 'I've had a great week, scoring for my country then twice for my club,' said Gray. 'I've never scored a hat-trick and I was possibly trying too hard, but to be honest as long as we are winning, I'm not bothered who scores the goals.'

For Dave Bassett it was the Sheffield United manager's second defeat at Roker Park in six months, the previous visit sparking off Peter Reid's managerial career with Sunderland:

Coming to Sunderland was always going to be a difficult fixture for us. We will play worse than that away from home and get a result. Sunderland probably only had two or three players different from the side that beat us near the end of last season. It's just sometimes when you are at the top, players are a bit more confident and get the breaks. Peter Reid has got Sunderland off to a good start and I saw some of those players last season when they were not so confident.

Sunderland in fact oozed confidence in the early stages of the midweek trip to the Victoria Ground, only to pay the penalty for a series of missed chances and slump to a first defeat in 12 League games against a Stoke City side destined to reach the play-offs. But a bigger blow than the chance to draw level on points with second-placed Leicester City was the loss of Paul Bracewell early in the second-half. Manager Peter Reid's right-hand man, so influential in the first-half of the campaign, faced up to the 14th operation of his career. It emerged he had played through the pain barrier since the start of the season and was prepared to wait until the close season for further surgery. Reid commented:

> I've known about it for the last six to eight weeks. That's the biggest compliment I can pay to Paul Bracewell. About four weeks ago he gave the ball away, so I knew there must be something wrong. It's something at the back of your mind, but you try and shut it out. He is a lad I have played with and against and he is a fine footballer. He is a great influence but it's just one of those things that happen in football. You don't pull Paul Bracewell off unless he is really struggling. He didn't want to come off, but there was no point leaving him on as he couldn't turn. He's been playing through it, but that's the end and he will need a hernia operation.

Sunderland stayed in the Midlands after the midweek defeat to prepare for the match against West Brom at the Hawthorns, but there was a further blow on arrival at the ground when David Kelly failed a fitness test on a calf injury. But Lee Howey, deputising for the unlucky Kelly, proved a match-winning replacement with a tenth-minute header to settle another intense and hard-fought encounter. Peter Reid was more pleased with the three points than the performance and revealed he had given his players a verbal rocket during the interval:

'The first 45 minutes is the worst we have played,' he said. 'I don't think it, I know it. So it was pleasing that we dug a way out and scratched a result. You can't play well all the time, but defensively I thought we were all over the place. We played better at Stoke and did not get a result. Sometimes in games you are going to have to dig and defend, and when they put the pressure on, we stood up to it.'

Bracewell headed off to a Harley Street clinic determined to bounce back ahead of schedule from another set-back. 'I've known since pre-season, even before the rest of the squad came back, that I had a problem,' he said. 'I had an injection and after one of the midweek games the specialist confirmed that I needed an operation and he said he would do it the next day. But I wanted to play on as long as possible as we were in a good run and doing well. The pain has been bearable but it got to the stage in the Stoke City game where I could not continue.'

Top of the First Division at the end of November:

	P	W	D	L	F	A	Pts
1 Millwall	19	9	7	3	23	17	34
2 Norwich City	19	9	6	4	30	20	33
3 Grimsby Town	19	9	6	4	23	19	33
4 Leicester City	19	9	5	5	31	26	32
5 Birmingham	19	8	7	4	30	22	31
6 Sunderland	18	8	7	3	21	15	31

Bracewell was on his way back from London when the club was rocked by a written transfer request from Phil Gray. And Reid, in no mood to tolerate players prepared to rock the boat, had no hesitation in agreeing to inform clubs of the availability of the Northern Ireland international. 'Phil Gray handed in a written transfer request and reluctantly it will be granted,' said Reid. 'I do not want anybody who does not want to play for this club. It's up to him, but if I get an offer which I think is acceptable, he can go. His contract is up at the end of the season and he came to see me a few weeks ago about a new deal. We talked about it, but I said the way the club is at the moment, I would prefer he left it for the time being.'

Gray had believed talks with previous manager Mick Buxton would lead to an improved deal, and as he had not been able to make any progress with new boss Reid, he wanted to force the issue. Premiership giants Everton and Aston Villa were expected to lead the chase for the services of Sunderland's top goalscorer of the last two seasons. Both West Ham and Southampton had made approaches the previous season only to be frightened off by the then asking price of £2 million.

Gray's insistence on a new deal cost him his place for another live televised match, the return against Crystal Palace. Sunderland were far from their Sunday best when completing the double over the fancied Londoners to draw level with Millwall at the top of the table. If television viewers were not treated to a classic, at least they witnessed the type of gutsy and committed performance often needed to win promotion. Martin Scott's 39th-minute penalty settled another dour struggle as Sunderland again failed to produce their attractive style of play in front of the TV cameras. But a record of fewer defeats by any other side and a defensive record bettered by none are testimony to the joint leaders' promotion credentials. 'We are up there but there's a long way to go,' said Reid. 'You've got to battle your way through a season sometimes and that typifies a team who have got hopes of going up.' On his decision to leave out Gray, he said: 'As a manager you make decisions and, on the day, that was the one I went with. I make decisions on the whole focus of the club and my own idea of how I want the club to be run.'

The following night, at ten past ten of all times, a spiced-up draw was made for the third round of the FA Cup with former Manchester United goalscoring hero Denis Law and England coach Terry Venables pulling out the numbers. To land another mouth-watering tie away to the favourites Manchester United was to prove another exciting chapter in a memorable season.

Sunderland should have faced a demanding six-match League programme before the Old Trafford tie but the weather was to wreck havoc with the fixture list in the build-up to tackling Eric Cantona *et al* in their own back-yard. Perhaps it was the thought of lining up against the star-studded Reds which prompted Phil Gray to issue a statement on his reasons for submitting a transfer request:

I consider my time at Sunderland to be the most enjoyable of my career and I feel I am playing at my peak. If the club were to offer me a new contract, I would give it very serious consideration. I am now entering the last six months of my current contract with Sunderland. During the last two and a half years I have enjoyed a happy relationship with the club, its management and especially the fans. I have never given less than 100 per cent either on or off the field. However, as my playing contract expires in June 1996 and no offer of a new contract has been made, I feel it in my best interests to seek a new club now. This is in no way a reflection on anybody in the club and I can assure everyone that I will continue to do my best at all times.

With Kelly ruled out through injury, Gray was recalled to form a new-look strike force with Craig Russell for the top-of-the-table clash with Millwall. The six-goal thrashing of the leaders was sensational. Martin Scott opened the floodgates with a 15th-minute penalty but the star of the show was Russell. The young striker bagged four of the goals with Gray also getting in on the act in the amazing goal-scoring spree.

Russell couldn't even force his way into the side at the start of the season but here he was blasting his way into the record books. Only 13 other players have achieved the feat for the club, the last being Eric Gates in the 7–0 thrashing of Southend in the 1987/88 Third Division Championship season. He joined Roker immortals John Campbell, Bobby Gurney, George Holley, Dave Halliday, James Richardson, Charlie Buchan, Raich Carter, Trevor Ford, Johnny Millar, Jackie Robinson, Ronnie Turnbull and Stan Cummins. Only Buchan, Gurney and Cummins have scored five goals in a match and Russell, by his own admission, should have joined the all-time greats:

It was just one of those things. People say strikers miss the easiest ones and it was proven against Millwall. That was only my second game playing through the middle, but it's even more frustrating when you are not in the side.

But it's been a great day and my happiest moment in football. Not many players score four goals in a match and I am pleased to be one of them. It's a plus point for me and it's up to me to keep going. The gaffer will put me in if he thinks it right and perhaps I haven't done as well as I could when I have played out wide this season. The gaffer thinks my best position is through the middle, but he asked me to play wide as he thinks I can get a few goals for him.

Manager Reid paid tribute to Russell's goalscoring spree, but took even greater satisfaction from the fact that the 11 players involved in the rout of the previous League leaders were at the club last season:

The lads out there were the same as finished last season fifth from bottom. That speaks volumes for those players. I thought the confidence coming off the terraces was instilled in the players as well. I've spoken once or twice that we have been threatening a performance like that and, unfortunately for Millwall, they were on the end of it.

We are top of the league with a game in hand, so we are in an excellent position. You don't get there if you don't deserve it. We have set our standards and we have got to keep them. The quality of some of the goals was first class.

What Sunderland would have given for just one of Russell's goals a week later at Reading. Martin Smith eased the Roker men into a 13th-minute lead but Reading player-manager Jimmy Quinn came off the substitute's bench to score a superb 86th-minute equaliser, and two minutes later he thumped a header against the bar. Derby closed to within a point by winning 1–0 at Millwall to set up a cracker between the teams at the Baseball Ground the next Saturday. Quinn, however, believed his late intervention only temporarily checked Sunderland's march towards the Premiership:

I would not say they are the best team in the division – but I would say nobody is better. I have played against Sunderland several times over the years and that is the best team I have come up against. They are well organised, they battle for each other and they have the ability now to go away from home and grind out a result.

If they are top of the First Division in the second week in January, I would fancy them to go up, because things will then snowball for them. We have played all the teams at the top and I think Sunderland have as good a chance as anyone on their display against us. They will win more games than they lose. Peter Reid has got them battling and they are prepared to fight to the end for a result.

Quinn was also convinced that deep down his Northern Ireland international colleague Phil Gray wanted to be part of Sunderland's success. 'I know Phil loves Sunderland and doesn't really want to leave. I think he is just after a better contract and now the club is doing so well, I don't think he wants to be going. He is a fantastic player and if I had a couple of million pounds to spend, I would not hesitate to go for him. Phil is not a prolific goalscorer, but he is such a lively player, he is one of the kingpins of the Sunderland side.'

The on-off loan transfer of Chelsea utility player Gareth Hall was finally given the green light with the Welsh international turning his back on the bright lights of London for a fresh start on the north-east coast.

No stranger to big games between the clubs – he played in the sixth-round FA Cup-tie in 1992 – Hall had first-hand knowledge of the famous Roker Roar:

> I played in the first game at Stamford Bridge and was on the substitutes bench for the replay at Roker Park when the atmosphere was the best I have ever experienced. Our manager Ian Porterfield always told the players if you get the chance to move to Sunderland, take it. He was always talking about Sunderland and its supporters.
>
> I am excited. London is all well and good but in football terms, it really is an exciting time for this area. I am only 26 and have had some good years at Chelsea. But I am out of contract and I was looking to move on. I was given the chance to come to the north-east which, at the moment, is the place to be. Sunderland look as though they are ready to follow in the footsteps of the other two even if there is still a long way to go.

Reid was delighted to welcome the newcomer aboard for an initial month on loan with a view to a permanent £300,000 move. He said: 'It's always nice when people from big clubs like Chelsea want to come north. Everything has been very positive and I am delighted to get him. He is a Premiership player who can operate in a number of positions. He is the type of player I like. I have spoken to people who have worked with the lad and have received good reports.'

Hall had to settle for a place on the substitutes bench for another top-of-the-table clash, against second-placed Derby County at the Baseball Ground. Sunderland were given a taste of their own medicine, losing 3–1 and the top spot to the Rams. Michael Gray's 34th-minute lead was wiped out by former Roker golden boy Marco Gabbiadini; Dutch international Ronnie Willems scored from a disputed penalty and Dean Sturridge put the issue beyond doubt in the last few minutes to chalk up a seventh win in eight matches.

Worse was to follow, though, as Sunderland were caught up by the big freeze with three successive matches called off. First casualty was the home game with Grimsby Town on Boxing Day and Derby County took full advantage, winning 1–0 at Huddersfield to go four points clear at the top and a further point ahead of Sunderland. A big snow-clearing operation swung into action in an all-out effort to beat the freeze for the all-ticket clash visit of Birmingham, but again all to no avail. Derby's visit to Watford was another of the games to suffer the same fate to leave only four points separating the second- and 11th-placed teams. Only three matches survived, none involving the promotion contenders, leaving Sunderland still five points adrift of the leaders. Top of the First Division table at the end of December read:

		P	W	D	L	F	A	Pts
1	Derby County	24	12	7	5	39	28	43
2	Charlton	24	10	9	5	31	24	39
3	Birmingham	24	10	8	6	34	30	38
4	Sunderland	22	10	8	4	30	19	38

Instead of travelling to Oldham Athletic on New Year's Day to complete the halfway stage of the season, Sunderland were again left kicking their heels when Boundary Park became the first of another glut of casualties. The postponement was another blow, however, with Derby stretching their lead to eight points by beating Norwich City thanks to Marco Gabbiadini's last-minute winner. Both Leicester City and Huddersfield took advantage of Sunderland's inactivity to push Reid's side into sixth place.

5

A New Year Draught

Alex Ferguson is now among the top five managers in the history of the English game after Manchester United's historic second double. His tally of six major triumphs – three League championships and three FA Cups – has been bettered only by his late Old Trafford mentor Sir Matt Busby and Liverpool's Bob Paisley, sadly mourned this last season.

The Reds manager has won 11 pieces of silver since he was appointed to the Old Trafford hot seat in November 1986, including a League Cup, a European Cup Winners' Cup, the Super Cup and two Charity Shields. When his record in Scotland is added, his achievements are almost unsurpassable: three Scottish Premier titles, four Scottish Cups (including his first double in 1984), a League Cup and a first Cup Winners' Cup in 1983.

But Sunderland were just ten minutes away from dumping the favourites out of the FA Cup in their own back-yard until Eric Cantona, who else, popped up with a headed equaliser to the dismay of more than 8,000 passionate Roker fans who had out-shouted the Old Trafford faithful.

Sunderland welcomed back Paul Bracewell, out for seven weeks after a hernia operation, skipper Kevin Ball from suspension and David Kelly from injury, and though United gambled on the fitness of Gary Pallister and Steve Bruce and full-back Denis Irwin, there was no place for injured goalkeeper Peter Schmeichel. Peter Reid gained a psychological advantage half an hour before the start by milking the applause of the fans and the ploy had an immediate effect on his players. United, however, survived an early onslaught and when Nicky Butt lobbed Alec Chamberlain after 13 minutes, the script was going to plan. But not even the loss of Ball midway through the half shattered Sunderland's belief, and it was no surprise when substitute Steve Agnew equalised. Two minutes later Craig Russell silenced the Stretford End with a well-taken goal but Cantona, as so often throughout United's double season, had the last word.

Ferguson admitted his side was fortunate to have had a second bite of the cherry: 'We were lucky to get a second chance, but that illustrates what the Cup is all about. There's always an element of luck. We carried it with us and hopefully we will be in the next round too. Sunderland had two lively strikers in Craig Russell and Phil Gray, who chased everything, so it was a good game for them, even though they tired towards the end. The backing from the Sunderland fans was incredible. Their fabulous, fanatical support was worth an extra man to their side.' Peter Reid summed up the mood in the Sunderland camp:

> I've got a disappointed dressing room and that's the way I feel. It speaks volumes for the performance when you've got a disappointed dressing room. When you come to a place like this and don't stick your chances away, you think you have lost your chance.
>
> I did think we had blown it, but, at the same time, I knew we could cause them problems and, if you keep playing like that, at the end of the day you get your just rewards. They've got some quality players and the movement for the first goal was excellent. But I couldn't see them getting back in at 2–1. I am a bit disappointed, but that's football. Even though we have got a draw, I think we did enough to win it.

Rearranging three outstanding League games and slotting the replay into a crowded fixture list did Sunderland no favours. Their plight was not helped when the home League game with Norwich was switched to the Sunday for live television.

Sky added extra pressure with their demands to screen the replay

48 hours later; they were committed to showing England's one-day cricket international against South Africa on the Wednesday night and Sunderland were not in a position to turn their back on the £60,000 television fee. Club secretary Paul Fiddaman commented: 'There was no pressure put on us to switch the Cup game. But it makes sound sense from a cash point of view.'

In days of old Cup replays were played the following week but Alex Ferguson and his right-hand man Brian Kidd took advantage of the modern arrangements of at least ten days' grace to be among the guests in the director's box for the visit of Norwich City. They slept more easily in their beds after watching Sunderland slump to a disappointing home defeat, only the second and last in the League for the season. Ashley Ward's 12th-minute goal was enough for Gary Megson to celebrate his first win in 12 games as manager of the Canaries with Reid offering no excuses: 'It's a disappointing result, but we've just got to bounce back. They defended with numbers in depth and we were not good enough to break them down. All credit to Norwich.'

Derby's 3–0 over Reading stretched their lead over second placed Charlton to nine points with Sunderland slipping to eighth place, a staggering 11 points behind Jim Smith's side. Top of the First Division at the halfway stage read:

		P	W	D	L	F	A	Pts
1	Derby County	26	14	7	5	44	29	49
2	Charlton	25	11	9	5	35	27	42
3	Huddersfield	27	11	8	8	37	32	41
4	Stoke City	26	10	9	7	37	32	39
5	Leicester City	25	10	8	7	40	36	38
6	Norwich City	27	10	8	9	39	36	38
7	Birmingham	25	10	8	7	37	34	38
8	Sunderland	23	10	8	5	30	20	38

Promotion again took a back seat as Cup fever swept Wearside: the eagerly awaited re-match with Alex Ferguson's star-studded team. Peter Reid was looking forward to it. 'I can't wait. The problem against Norwich was we got a bit anxious but that's football and I had a funny feeling about that one.' United were without suspended David

Beckham and injured central defender Gary Pallister, but they welcomed back Peter Schmeichel. Ferguson sprang a surprise by switching to a five-man defence with Paul Parker in the role of sweeper. The old cliché 'a game of two halves' was never more appropriate with Schmeichel United's hero, even though he was beaten by Phil Gray's 24th-minute strike. But when Ferguson ditched his defensive formation during the interval, bringing on Paul Scholes for the hapless Parker, the Reds were a totally different outfit. Scholes grabbed a 70th-minute equaliser and as the pressure mounted, a last-gasp headed winner from Andy Cole was a cruel blow even though Sunderland had been reduced to chasing shadows. United were awesome in the second period. Reid was adamant the bubble hadn't burst after three defeats in four matches had cost his side top spot in the League and an exit from the major cup competition at the first hurdle.

He rapped out a defiant message to the doubters:

> We've got to keep it going. The fans witnessed a performance against Manchester United that we will try and give them week in week out. It's a big plus to have 21,000 fans out there. It helps to create a great atmosphere and we will need them in the next few weeks. If we perform like that we will win games. They are all big games coming up and we must start winning again. Over the two ties we have had a good go, but we just didn't do it. All credit to Manchester United. They have pushed us back in the second-half and we did not hold the ball up enough up front against a side full of quality.
>
> We are out of the Cup and the best of luck to Manchester United. We have got to look to the League, and I have always said that is the most important. You never look back. We lost a close Cup-tie, but at times we were chasing shadows.

The club launched a Key Plan part-season ticket designed to cope with a surge of demand for the remainder of the campaign. Fans worried about the prospect of being locked out of Roker Park were also given priority for away matches where admittance would be even more limited. The cost of the ticket was based on the face value of a match-day ticket and the response was staggering. 'We envisage

Peter Reid sounds the battle cry from day one in the fight for First Division survival against Sheffield United at Roker Park on 1 April 1995.

Flying High. Craig Russell gives Peter Reid a flying start to his Sunderland managerial career with a last-gasp winner against Sheffield United at Roker Park on 1 April 1995.

Sunderland defender Andy Melville celebrates his eighth-minute goal in the 2–0 win over Wolves at Roker Park on 26 August 1995.

Goalkeeper Alec Chamberlain dives full length to deny Wolves striker Steve Bull in Sunderland's 2–0 win over Wolves at Roker Park on 26 August 1995.

Phil Gray flings himself full length to head home a late equaliser against Huddersfield Town at the Sir Alfred MacAlpine Stadium on 21 October 1995.

Lee Howey stoops to head home the winning goal in Sunderland's 2–1 win over Barnsley at Roker Park on 28 October 1995.

Delight for Sunderland striker David Kelly as Phil Gray's shot beats Sheffield United goalkeeper Alan Kelly in the 2–0 win at Roker Park on 18 November 1995.

Lee Howey   his tenth-minute winner against West Brom at the Hawthorns on 25 November 1995.

Craig Russell celebrates his fourth goal in the six-goal rout of Millwall at Roker Park on 9 December 1995.

Sunderland captain Kevin Ball thumps a header against the Charlton Athletic bar in a goalless draw at Roker Park on 8 April 1996.

Craig Russell fires through a crowded Derby County goalmouth to complete the scoring in a 3–0 win over the First Division leaders at Roker Park on 9 March 1996.

Michael Bridges squeezes ahead of colleague Paul Stewart to head home the winner against Huddersfield Town at Roker Park on 30 March 1996.

Shay Given kept 12 clean sheets in 17 appearances for Sunderland in a three-month loan spell from Blackburn Rovers.

Craig Russell . . . Sunderland's leading goalscorer with a tally of 14.

Goalkeeper Alec Chamberlain and skipper Kevin Ball in the lap of honour with the First Division Championship trophy at Roker Park on 27 April 1996.

Skipper Kevin Ball (left) and assistant manager Paul Bracewell proudly display the First Division Championship trophy.

many of our games to be all-ticket for our supporters,' said chief executive John Fickling. 'That is a nuisance and, to avoid supporters having to make an extra trip to the ground for every match, we have introduced the Key Plan. We have to be fair to those people who put their money up front before the start of the season, but we feel this is a fair deal.'

Reid made a sensational swoop for Blackburn Rovers goalkeeper Shay Given as his battered side faced up to the live television cameras for a third successive match. The 19-year-old was signed on a month's loan while Gareth Hall put pen to paper on a £300,000 permanent move from Chelsea on the eve of the trip to Filbert Street to play Leicester City. All other teams in the First Division had been in action 24 hours earlier and Sunderland slipped to tenth position on goal difference. A point from a goalless draw was enough to climb three positions, but not without mixed fortunes for the two newcomers. Given kept a clean sheet after a nervous start, but Hall was sent off for two bookable offences.

Peter Reid said he would consider making an appeal on behalf of the Welsh international, who accepted the decision of Stoke referee Jim Rushton in his stride: 'I was sent off a few years ago against Everton but this was a lot harder to take because of the circumstances. When the referee came up to me he said, "Look, I have got to be consistent." It's not the best of starts, but I am not going to let it affect me.'

Richard Ord's goals are few and far between so, when the centre-back cracked home a 64th-minute winner against Grimsby Town in the start to clearing up the backlog of fixtures, he had good reason to celebrate. His goal ended a run of six matches without a win. The stand-in skipper said: 'That's got to be the most important goal of my career. It gets us back up there. To be honest I should have scored more goals than I have. I've been a bit unlucky, I must have hit the woodwork a dozen times, but I'm a big lad and I've got to make my presence felt in both penalty areas.'

Reid ensured he took full advantage of the loan system to pounce for Manchester United winger Terry Cooke on the eve of the re-arranged home game with Tranmere Rovers. The 19-year-old scored the winning penalty which clinched the FA Youth Cup for Manchester United and Reid looked to one of the finest young prospects in the country to give him width on the right. Brett Angell, very much an outcast under Reid's regime, joined Sheffield United on a month's loan even though Sunderland lagged behind their promotion rivals in the goalscoring stakes. Goalscoring again proved a problem against Tranmere; the consolation from a goalless draw was Sunderland's move into third place, still seven points behind Derby with a game in hand.

Only half a dozen goals had been scored in eight League and Cup games since the six-hit show against Millwall, but the directors made it perfectly clear to the manager there was no further cash to give the side a badly needed injection of goalscoring power. Said Reid: 'I've got until the third week in March to make any further loan signings, and if a quality player becomes available, I will try to bring him in. It's no use moaning about injuries, you get injuries in football and have just got to deal with them. Like any other manager, I want to improve the squad, but it's a little bit difficult at the moment.'

Top of the First Division at the end of January read:

		P	W	D	L	F	A	Pts
1	Derby County	27	14	8	5	45	30	50
2	Charlton	26	12	9	5	39	28	45
3	Sunderland	26	11	10	5	31	28	43
4	Huddersfield	28	11	9	8	37	32	42

A crunching 3–0 defeat at Wolves sent Sunderland tumbling down to fifth place and the gap at the top increased to six points with former Roker star Don Goodman in the thick of the action. A controversial penalty awarded against Lee Howey for a challenge on Goodman led to Andy Thompson becoming the first player to find a way past Given in the youngster's fourth match. Goodman added a second goal a few minutes later, and when Mark Atkins headed home on the hour, there was no way back. Goodman, however, backed his ex-colleagues to be in the promotion frame as soon as the strikers rediscovered their goalscoring touch:

Phil Gray and Craig Russell are quality players. I am not bothered how many goals they have scored, but, as long as they keep their heads up and keep going, I am sure the goals will come. Sunderland have been scrapping for goals and they haven't been going in. But all it needs is for somebody to score a couple and spark it off again. They have been doing very well defensively as everybody knows and not scoring enough goals as everybody knows. I don't think there is much difference between the third top and third bottom in this League, but Sunderland are a very good team – even though they never really threatened us.

Not surprisingly Reid was linked with experienced strikers to prop up the promotion challenge with former Roker idol Ally McCoist, Chris Waddle and Northern Ireland international Niall Quinn in the frame. But all the manager was prepared to discuss was a possible loan deal: 'I have looked to Europe to bring players in on loan. I've spoken to a few players but have not been able to clinch anything yet. I will keep on working and trying.'

Nothing materialised before the home game against Port Vale, though Dariusz Kubicki made his 100th consecutive appearance for the club at right-back. He was the first Sunderland player to achieve this feat since goalkeeper Barry Siddall played in 103 successive matches between October 1976, when he replaced Jimmy Montgomery, and February 1979. The Polish international played 15 games on loan at the end of the 1993/94 season before completing a £100,000 move from Aston Villa. He was an ever-present in the 51 League and Cup games the following season and had no rival for the right-back position. His run during the championship-winning season reached a total of 118 games on the trot.

No real damage was done by another disappointing goalless home draw as Derby County also shared a stalemate with Wolves at the Baseball Ground. The excitement for a near 16,000 crowd was the introduction of 17-year-old Michael Bridges for an out-of-sorts Phil Gray. The teenager walked away with three man-of-the-match sponsor awards for his half-hour super show, a sad reflection on the rest of his team-mates. Peter Reid admitted he had been forced to introduce the club's latest prospect ahead of schedule because of the goal drought. But the confident Bridges had the talent and the temperament to develop into an exciting player.

If he works hard and keeps his feet firmly on the ground, I think he could have a future. He's got a lovely touch and he's one of the those players who is quite deceptive because he has got pace. The lad has done ever so well since he came to the club. He has progressed through the youths, but last year he was still playing in schools football. Phil Gray is going through one of those spells that some strikers go through in their careers, so I decided to make a change. But sometimes, when you are asking a 17-year-old to start, it's a bit difficult.

Gray was relegated to substitute for one of the longest trips of the season to Portsmouth with young Bridges again on the bench and Lee Howey deputising for the suspended Richard Ord in central defence. Steve Agnew put Sunderland ahead, Hall equalised for the home side, and when Griffiths forced the ball over the line in 86 minutes, Sunderland were staring defeat in the face. Howey came to the rescue with an injury-time equaliser. The draw was to have a startling effect on the rest of the season. Derby's 2–1 victory at Southend opened up a ten-point gap with second-placed Charlton five points clear of Stoke City, Huddersfield and Sunderland.

Craig Russell left Fratton Park holding his head in his hands after Pompey keeper Alan Knight had saved his weak penalty kick. It was the sixth miss out of nine attempts from the penalty spot. Said Russell: 'It was just one of those things. I would have no worries about taking a penalty again – the best players in the world have missed penalties. I hit the target but the goalkeeper guessed right. Another day he might have gone the other way.' Peter Reid was more concerned at the goals his side conceded: 'If you score two goals away from home – especially the way we defend – you expect to win. The first goal was sloppy and the second one was even worse. I've been getting sick of coming into press conferences and saying the same old thing: that we've been the better side but just haven't come away with the three points.'

Howey's reward for his last-gasp goal was to switch up front to make way for the return of Ord from suspension for the home game with Ipswich Town. Sunderland survived a snowstorm and an Ipswich blitz to move into third position, and if Craig Russell was the goalscoring hero, Shay Given deserved all the accolades which came his way. The 3–0 defeat at Portman Road still rankles with Peter Reid. His side had completely outplayed Ipswich only to return home empty-handed. The Roker manager, therefore, had no sympathy for George Burley's beaten side as they left the north-east for the long trek back to East Anglia. Even the most biased Sunderland supporter would agree Ipswich would have won at a canter if early chances had been converted. Ipswich carved out half a dozen reasonable openings in the first ten minutes, but were either denied by the heroics of Given or let down by woeful finishing.

There was no sympathy from Reid: 'I would not say we were lucky. If you are going to get promoted you have got to be mentally strong. Over the next few weeks that is going to be tested and hopefully we will get through that. I am delighted with the three points when we were second best for long spells against a side from last season's Premiership. We have dug in and, at the end of the day, kept a clean sheet which was very important. It's swings and roundabouts because we did play better at Portman Road and got a 3–0 hiding.' Rarely do managers come up with the same assessment but Burley, not surprisingly, was in full agreement: 'I felt we dominated from start to finish. We played some good stuff but it was one of those games where we have created as many chances as I have known this season, but we just could not score. We have scored 50 goals this season and, while I couldn't ask for any more in attitude and commitment, I just thought the killer instinct was missing.'

It was another of the relegated clubs, however, who had crept up on the rails. Crystal Palace, rejuvenated under new manager Dave Bassett, were emerging as a real threat to the promotion contenders. Palace, unbeaten, since losing at Roker Park on 3 December, overturned a 2–0 deficit to win 3–2 at Tranmere to move into contention. Paul Bracewell warned of the dangers on the eve of the visit of Luton Town, who stretched an unbeaten run under new manager Lennie Lawrence to nine matches after an impressive midweek draw against Derby County at the Baseball Ground: 'There tends to be a reaction when a new manager comes in, but Lennie Lawrence is very experienced and he has been in the game a long time. I don't suppose it's surprised a lot of people in the game how well he has done. Luton are the in-form team at the moment, after looking to be dead and buried at one stage.' The fact Sunderland needed the help of a bizarre own goal to emerge with all three points proved Bracewell's point. Central defender Julian James headed a Michael

Gray centre into his own net in a game short of clear-cut chances.

Derby gained maximum points from the visit of Portsmouth, Charlton were held at Oldham but Crystal Palace slipped back into the pack after losing 3–0 at Huddersfield.

Peter Reid was again more delighted with the result than the performance as his side opened up a seven-point cushion for a play-off place: 'At this stage of the season, you take anything that is going. I am delighted with the victory and the players worked hard again. I wouldn't say it was our greatest performance, but against a team that has done ever so well recently, I thought we were solid through the middle.' Lawrence was in an ideal position to assess the promotion credentials of Sunderland and Derby County, and commented:

> I would say Sunderland were more solid and Derby had more attacking flair. I think, when you have won twice at home and not played as well as you can, it's a great sign for Sunderland. I think they are an absolute certainty for a top-six place and I would not write them off for second spot. But, if I had to put my money on who will finish top, I would go for Derby. Peter Reid needs to buy a striker, everybody knows that. I've only seen Charlton once and they've got a lot of young players and I don't know how they will cope. It's who copes with the run-in really, who can grind results out when not playing well. Sunderland have certainly done that.

Manchester United's reluctance to extend the loan period of Terry Cooke as Sunderland took to the air for the midweek game against Southend United at Roots Hall paved the way for Steve Agnew to return to the side. But it was young Michael Bridges who was as high as a kite when the squad left less than an hour later for the return journey from a fog-bound Southend airport.

While the rest of the party cast doubts over whether the flight would be aborted because of the weather conditions, the youngster was on cloud nine, celebrating a sensational substitute appearance. The rookie striker scored just 12 seconds after replacing Lee Howey to seal a third win in eight days – in only his fourth appearance as a substitute. The posse of journalists seeking a brief interview with Sunderland's whiz-kid had to seek out a protective manager before the youngster was able to give his views on his startling impact on a game the majority of fans could barely follow because of the fog.

Martin Scott had tucked away a penalty and Bridges added to the lead, but many left the ground unaware of the goalscorers. A couple of fans on the London Underground the next morning overheard our conversation on the way to King's Cross and joined in the conversation. They were grateful to be filled in of the details as they were behind the goal at the opposite end where Scott and Bridges were on target. Said Bridges: 'It's a dream come true – I can't believe it. I'm over the moon, it's the best feeling in the world.' Reid was just as enthusiastic: 'Michael has got an eye for goal. He has got a chance, but I don't want to put him under pressure. You can see from his build that he has not filled out. We have got to treat him gently and it's up to us, as a football club, to look after him. He finishes like that all the time and full credit to him. I want to stick to the policy of playing him as a substitute, but, if he keeps scoring goals, he will put pressure on people. That's something I don't mind.'

Top of the First Division at the end of February:

		P	W	D	L	F	A	Pts
1	Derby County	32	16	11	5	52	35	59
2	Sunderland	32	14	12	6	37	25	54
3	Charlton	31	13	13	5	45	33	52
4	Huddersfield	31	13	10	8	43	34	49
5	Stoke City	31	13	10	8	43	34	49

6

The Rokermen Gather Pace

Sunderland have never been at their best in live television games, with a run of six successive defeats enough to make them camera-shy. West Ham, Leicester City, Barnsley and Newcastle all emerged victorious in the 1992/93 season. Crystal Palace and Middlesbrough extended the run a year later before the tables were turned on the Boro.

In the following season a 2–2 draw was followed by the 4–1 FA Cup defeat by a Jürgen Klinsmann-inspired Tottenham Hotspur and Tranmere Rovers and Grimsby Town in the league. The 1995/96 season was marginally better with a 1–0 win over Crystal Palace the only maximum return from five appearances on live television.

Derby had extended their lead to nine points by beating Huddersfield Town on the Saturday, and though Charlton Athletic went down at Portsmouth, Stoke City's home win over Barnsley moved Lou Macari's side to within a couple of points of an automatic promotion place when Sunderland travelled to Cleethorpes for another Sunday showdown.

Sunderland made a mockery of both their abysmal TV record and goalscoring problems to romp to a convincing four-goal win with Bridges again getting in on the act as a late goalscoring substitute. A first goal in 14 months for skipper Kevin Ball set Sunderland on their way but it was not until Craig Russell took advantage of a dreadful mix-up in the Grimsby Town defence that Roker's army of supporters could relax. Late strikes from Phil Gray and Bridges stamped the seal of approval on the win. Peter Reid, however, agreed that his side was flattered by the margin of victory:

> I don't think it was one of our best performances of the season. We were slightly fortunate at half-time to come in one-up, but what pleases me is we are getting results at a critical stage of the season. It's another clean sheet and an added bonus is the goals at the end.
>
> The scoreline flattered us immensely, but we have come off this season when we have not got what we deserved in other games. In some games we created chances and did not do ourselves justice, but I am delighted that we have stuck the ball in the back of the net. I wouldn't call us a promotion team at the moment. We are in with a shout when we have not being playing well.

With a crunch game on the horizon against Derby County, Paul Stewart joined the promotion ranks until the end of the season on a free transfer from Liverpool. The former England international, a £2.3 million transfer from Tottenham Hotspur two years previously, was brought in to give the attack a new dimension, though most of his games of late had been in midfield. Said Reid: 'I've kept tabs on him since he went back to Liverpool earlier in the season. I've got him on a free until the end of the season and if I can get Ian Rush on a free at the end of the season, I will be delighted. It's up to the lad but I am sure he will do well enough to get another contract.' Stewart was given a run-out in the reserves to prove his fitness and he quickly settled in again, delighted to be given another chance to prove he was far from finished:

> I've tried to keep myself as fit as possible, but under the circumstances, it's been very frustrating. An injury that was supposed to take two or three weeks to clear up has ended up taking six months. It's been a long road but I've got a chance and it's up to me to take it. My main concern was to get fit then worry if somebody like Peter Reid would come in for me. As far as I am concerned I have nothing to prove to anybody – only myself – and I know I can do it. I just want to be injury-free all the way along.

Peter Reid has been in touch with me all the way through the last six months, so it was nice that he has taken an interest and there was light at the end of the tunnel. I knew if, and when I got myself fit, there was no way back at Liverpool in the first team. Peter's interest kept me going because I did have a few low points, having been injured quite a bit over the last few years. I would be telling lies if I said I didn't want to play in the Premiership again. My first aim must be to help Sunderland win promotion then we'll see what happens about a further contract.

The arrival of Stewart pushed Brett Angell further down the batting order to the extent that the £600,000 outcast was transfer-listed and clubs were informed of his availability. Said Reid: 'Paul Stewart has come in, Michael Bridges has come through and I've also got Lee Howey, so his chances are very limited here. He has been on loan and scored goals, so we will wait and see what happens.' Angell accepted that his days were numbered, not having been with the first team since the opening weeks of the season. He said: 'Obviously I am disappointed that things have not worked out here but I feel, given the chance, I could have scored goals. The team has done ever so well and it's a shame not to be part of it. But, at the end of the day, I have to rebuild my career and unfortunately it's not going to be here. The club is going in the right direction, but I have no grudges to bear and must move on. I have not lost faith in my ability to score goals – given the chance.'

Stewart was not considered match-fit as Sunderland moved to within four points of leaders Derby County with two games in hand after inflicting a three-goal blitz on the Rams in the top-of-the-table clash watched by an all-ticket crowd just short of capacity. Derby, unbeaten in 20 games, were comprehensively outplayed with a double from Craig Russell and Steve Agnew's fourth goal of the campaign settling an absorbing match.

Former Roker goalscoring hero Marco Gabbiadini summed up the First Division title race:

It was quite an important game for both clubs, but losing is not the end of the world for us. I suppose, in a way, we will be relieved that the run is over. I can't see our club record of 20 unbeaten games being beaten for a long time and I think we had reached the stage where we were saying, 'let's go out and make sure we don't lose' rather than saying, 'let's go out and win.

I will be happy if both clubs go up at the end of the season. There's still a long way to go, but both clubs have the strength in depth and support to sustain a challenge. Sunderland work very hard and close teams down and took their goals well. They simply didn't let us settle when we had the ball. We thought if we could weather the storm for a bit we would be in with a chance, but that early goal made all the difference.

Peter Reid hailed the performance 'the best since I came here' without going overboard on his team's chances of promotion.

Beating Swindon last season was a big game, but that was the best because Derby are a good side. They are the best in the League. Tables do not lie. They are up there, but it was an excellent performance.

The League is so much up and down. I can remember Millwall being top when we played them here before Christmas. If you don't keep doing it, you can go up and down the League. Consistent football keeps you at the top and we've won five on the trot. They are all big games for us and we've got to make sure we keep on picking up the points. But I think we would have given most teams a game on Saturday.

Derby are very strong and will go close. I am hopeful we will go close as well. The fans have seen results in the past and not really believed. I think on the evidence of the Derby game, they will see we are not far off.

The fans were kept waiting until the 86th minute of a bitterly cold night at Boundary Park before the celebrations of a sixth successive victory could get underway. Kevin Ball headed Sunderland to within a point of Derby County with a game in hand after Mickey Gray's early opener had been cancelled out on the stroke of half-time by Lee Richardson.

Said Peter Reid: 'It's a lovely position to be in and it just shows what can happen when you win six games on the trot. Our supporters were superb and for three and a half thousand of them to get down from the north-east in difficult conditions, I hold my hands up to them. I'm delighted for them that we got the three points.'

Sunderland were again in demand by the television companies for the visit to the Midlands to take on Birmingham at St Andrew's. And they were given a pre-match boost when Derby County were held to a home draw by bottom-of-the-table Watford. And how they grabbed the chance to go top again – a position they sustained until the end of the season even though there were still ten games to go. Centre-back Andy Melville added to Steve Agnew's early opener with his fourth goal of the season: 'I came to Sunderland hoping they would soon be in the Premiership. I had one season at Swansea where we got in the play-offs through the back door, but this is my first real go at promotion. My job is to help us not concede goals and another clean sheet is very important. Scoring goals is all very nice but, to a defender, that's the icing on the cake.' Birmingham manager Barry Fry, never one to mince his words, predicted Sunderland would not only win the League quite handsomely, but that Peter Reid would become one of the best managers in the game:

> I can't praise the man enough. I can see Peter becoming a leading manager, but whether it's with Sunderland, I am not sure. They haven't got the financial clout to back him in the Premiership because I know he will want to have a go for honours.
>
> He's certainly done a marvellous job – no question about that at all. I think he went there when Sunderland were really struggling against relegation. He's introduced two or three players, but it's the same lads that are going to get up to the Premiership. Bracewell is different class and Stewart is very experienced. He's got a lovely blend of youth and experience and certainly has the boys believing in themselves. Sunderland have this great will-to-win and I can see them going on to win the league by ten points. But that doesn't help us. It was a great opportunity for us to show what we are made of and, to be honest, we were nothing. We were very poor and that's not taking anything away from Sunderland.
>
> They beat us from start to finish. They were more aggressive, more determined, they competed for everything, passed the ball around great and never gave up on anything. They always had

players supporting the man in possession and always had alternatives and the only mystery is how they only won 2–0, because they were different class compared to us. It was men against boys. In the last three games I thought we had come a long way, but if that's the top of the First Division, we are a million miles away.

There was no danger of Reid, looking down on the rest of the division, not keeping his feet firmly on the ground: 'It's nice to be top, but we've got to stay there now. It's now down to us whether we can handle it and I am sure the players will be able to. We've got a base in that we don't give many goals away and now we are scoring goals at the other end, it gives us confidence. It's a lovely feeling being top, but the hardest part is staying there. We are there and we've got to handle the pressure.'

Elsewhere, Dave Bassett's magnificent unbeaten start of seven wins and two draws hoisted Crystal Palace into third place as serious challengers to Sunderland and Derby County for the two automatic promotion places.

The boom for a slice of the action had caught the public's imagination with the Roker Park Ticket Office working 'round the clock' to deal with the demand for tickets. The success of the Key Plan part-season ticket accounted for 25 per cent of the ground's capacity and there was no let-up in the weeks ahead.

With David Kelly making slow progress from an ankle operation, Peter Reid suffered a further blow when he lost the services of another international for the rest of the season, Phil Gray travelling to London for a groin operation. With six of the last ten matches at home, the bookmakers had slashed the odds for Sunderland to win the First Division Championship to six to four on.

The success of the squad and a lack of cash, reduced Peter Reid to a mere spectator on the traditional mad scramble transfer-deadline day when many a player is bought or sold to prop up a relegation campaign or boost a promotion push. The Roker manager did boost the kitty by transferring Martin Gray to Oxford United for a fee of £100,000, and full-back John Kay, on the mend from a twice-broken leg, joined Shrewsbury Town on loan with a view to playing at Wembley in the final of the Auto Windscreens Shield.

Reid revealed he had made a last-ditch effort to add Chris Waddle to the ranks, contacting Sheffield Wednesday manager David Pleat only hours before the deadline. It was no secret he had been on the trail of Waddle since before a ball was kicked with either Pleat refusing to sell or the price considered unrealistic by Sunderland's manager.

'I tried to sign Chris Waddle on loan,' said Reid. 'I spoke to David Pleat and he said if he had another few points he would probably have let him go. The lads here have done brilliantly for me, but if things hadn't been going well I could have sent Chris on and asked him for a bit of magic to win the game for us.'

Sunderland left it late to keep the bandwagon rolling and clinch the club's best winning run of the twentieth century and the best sequence for 104 years. The overall record of 13 successive wins was established in the Championship-winning season of 1891/92. Since then, seven wins on the trot were achieved on only three different occasions. Martin Scott's 82nd-minute winner proved even more invaluable when it emerged Derby County had been beaten by Norwich City at Carrow Road and Crystal Palace had been held to a goalless home draw by Portsmouth. The lead therefore was stretched to four points.

Said Scott: 'That's the first goal I can ever remember scoring with my right foot, even from my schoolboy days. Everybody knows my right leg is only for standing on, but I've certainly got a trusty right foot now. The fans were shouting for me to get a penalty, but I've gone one better and scored a goal with my right foot. It's helped us out in our hour of need.'

Tony Norman shaped up to the task of denying his former Roker team-mates a ninth successive win when he made a rare appearance for Huddersfield Town. Snapped up on a free transfer by Brian Horton, the former Welsh international forecast he was in for a busy afternoon. 'It's great to be playing against Sunderland and I am looking forward to coming back to Roker Park. I've seen Sunderland's last two matches on television and, to be honest, I can't see them losing another game. Against Birmingham City it was one of the best professional performances from a team I have seen in ages. They just dominated from start to finish. Looking at the other teams in contention, they are the best in the division.'

Norman and his Huddersfield colleagues were just seven minutes away from springing the shock result of the day, but they reckoned without that young upstart Michael Bridges again. Rob Edwards fired Huddersfield into a 21st-minute lead, the first goal Shay Given conceded in eight home League games, and though Kevin Ball equalised three minutes later, the ten-men visitors were back in front early in the second-half. Ben Thornley, on loan from Manchester United, was dismissed for a second bookable offence, throwing the ball at Scunthorpe referee Neil Barry as the teams left the field. Only a minute before he had been booked for a foul. Bridges replaced Craig Russell in the 75th minute and stunned the visitors with two headers in a four-minute spell to clinch a ninth successive victory. Peter Reid again kept a tight reign on the youngster, insisting any interviews were conducted in his presence:

> You have got to be careful with young lads. He scored goals for you so you think of what is the best way to use him because of his physical attributes. At the moment he is not up to it. I will continue to use him in little bursts at this moment in time. He is very, very confident. He is a lovely mover and I like centre-forwards who get in the penalty box. Michael gets into goalscoring positions and I think he has the chance of being a very good player.
>
> To be fair to the kid, he was playing schoolboy football a year ago. The first time I saw him pre-season, we had a game and I thought 'Who is he?' He has developed well, but, when you look at him physically, he is not there yet. He works hard and he is a level-headed lad. The rest of the lads get into him a little bit, but he's a smashing kid.

The youngster can look after himself not only on the pitch, but off it too, as he likes to trade words with the waiting media. 'I'm still waiting to wake up. I'm just pleased that it's happening but it has taken me by surprise. I fully expected to be still downstairs with the YTS lads but while it's happened so quickly, I am enjoying it. My first goal for the club at Southend was the best yet but to score two at home, including the winner, was brilliant.'

Bridges was discovered by Jack Hixon, the same scout who unearthed Alan Shearer when playing for Wallsend Boys' Club. He is determined to model his career on the England ace and was delighted to receive a glowing tribute from his boyhood idol. Chris Waddle, another of his heroes, was among the crowd who witnessed the youngster's amazing performance. Bridges added: 'My dad was always encouraging me to be a Newcastle supporter, but I was always a Tottenham fan as a young lad. They had Glenn Hoddle and Chris Waddle in the team and Waddle was my hero because of his skill and ability. But I try to model my game on Alan Shearer. We were both discovered by Jack Hixon and I believe Shearer is the best striker in the country. If I can do as well as him, I will be well pleased.'

Derby kept up the pressure by beating Stoke City at home, and Crystal Palace's 4–1 win at Millwall pushed the one-time leaders a step closer to relegation.

Top of the First Division at the end of March:

		P	W	D	L	F	A	Pts
1	Sunderland	38	20	12	6	52	28	72
2	Derby County	39	18	14	7	59	43	68
3	Crystal Palace	39	17	14	8	58	42	65
4	Charlton	37	16	14	7	52	40	62

Three days later the action switched to Vicarage Road where former Watford manager Glenn Roeder warned of the dangers of top taking on bottom. Roeder, sacked to make way for the return of ex-England manager Graham Taylor, predicted a tough time ahead for the leaders: 'Sunderland won't find the pitch to their liking – it's not in good condition. Watford will be relying on scoring the first goal but, morale the way it is, Sunderland will be in the driving seat even though Watford have a habit of getting results under floodlights at Vicarage Road. Sunderland and Charlton are probably the best sides we have played this season. We got a 1–1 draw at Roker Park earlier in the season, but it was murder on the day. We were like the magpies – thieving a point.'

Twice in a commanding two-goal lead and on course for a club record tenth successive win, Sunderland had to settle for a point after a six-goal thriller. Steve Agnew opened the scoring after 16 minutes and two minutes later Kevin Ball increased the lead. Tommy Mooney pulled a goal back for the home side, but just before the interval,

Craig Russell restored the two-goal lead. Mooney scored again immediately on the resumption and after 75 minutes it was all to play for thanks to a back-headed goal from Craig Ramage. There were to be no heroics from super sub Michael Bridges but this was one match where there should have been no need for the raw teenager to come to the rescue.

Peter Reid could only shake his head in disbelief after the indifferent performance had cost his side two valuable points: 'For the first 45 minutes, I thought we were different class then we changed our spots at half-time. But that happens in football. The players have done tremendously well and worked hard but credit to Watford – they had a right go. We have been sloppy on the night. We are all human and we sometimes have off days, including me. I am happy with the position we are in.'

But with Derby County losing at Ipswich, the point mathematically improved Sunderland's position, to the disappointment of Derby manager Jim Smith. He said: 'It was disappointing with so much at stake. We would have been fortunate to have got away with anything. It is always difficult coming to Ipswich, and even more difficult if you don't play.' If Peter Reid was disappointed with the overall result, he was delighted with the performance of Paul Stewart, who was settling into the side in an attacking role. Said Reid: 'The lad is different class. He is a Premiership player and I thought his performance against Watford was magnificent and awesome. He causes defences problems and gives time for other players to get into the penalty box. The fact he hasn't scored goals for us doesn't bother me. He's getting stronger and done smashing for us. He's done what I thought he would – he hasn't surprised me.' Stewart, after so long in the wilderness at Anfield, was just grateful for the chance to prove he was far from finished:

It's very nice when the manager says things like that about you. I have lost a lot of time over the last four years through injuries and maybe I have not looked after myself as well as I should. Hopefully I can make up for lost time here, but I am just taking each game as it comes now.

I'm getting stronger. When you get to over 30, you have to look after yourself. I'm 31 and looking after myself off the field helps. I was going nowhere at Liverpool and that's nobody's fault at Liverpool. I am grateful for a fresh opportunity and I have always said I have the ability to play at the top level. I want to get back to what I am doing best. I got a bit lost at Liverpool and at the moment I am only here until the end of the season. There is nothing definite in the things I would like to do. Part of a striker's role is to score goals but against Watford I laid two on and that's given me as much satisfaction when you are top of the League.

I'm never going to be a prolific goalscorer, but I like to get the odd goal or two. If I am contributing and we win, that's all that matters. It's just disappointing not to have won. The way other results went, we could have been promoted at Easter. Now it's going to take a bit longer.

Picking the ball out of the net three times was a big shock to the system for Shay Given. In his last two matches he had been beaten twice against Huddersfield and conceded a double on his Republic of Ireland international début against Russia: 'Of course I am disappointed to concede seven goals in three games. I always want to keep a clean sheet, no matter who I am playing against. But playing for Ireland was just brilliant. I had expected to be playing in the Under-21 international in front of a small crowd, then Alan Kelly injured his back and I was called into the full squad. My family and friends were in Dublin and the crowd was over 41,000. It was a great experience and I would like to think I will be playing for my country again in the near future.'

For the second successive month, Peter Reid missed out on the Manager of the Month award despite guiding Sunderland to the top of the First Division. In February, Sheffield United's Howard Kendall pipped Reid to the honour when many thought the Roker manager had a better claim, and it seemed inconceivable he would not walk off with the March award after guiding his side to a five-point lead at the top of the table, on the back of a nine-match winning streak. The Football League announced Crystal Palace's Dave Bassett Manager of the Month for March. A Football League spokesman said: 'Peter Reid can count himself very unlucky not to have won. Sunderland had a great month, but, unfortunately, they played fewer games. Sunderland won all six of their games in March, but Crystal Palace played eight, won six and drew two, which gave them a couple more points.' If Peter Reid was huffed by the snub, he certainly didn't express any emotions: 'It ain't a problem. That's football isn't it? Good luck to Mr Bassett. I'll tell you something, though, I wouldn't mind winning the award next month.'

Sunderland were allocated an extra 2,000 tickets for the visit to Barnsley and an estimated 8,000 prepared for one of the shortest trips of the season, a mere 240-mile round journey.

Barnsley manager Danny Wilson shaped up to the task of halting the red-and-white army on Easter Saturday, declaring: 'We're under no illusions about how difficult it is going to be. I wouldn't say Sunderland were the best side in the League yet – there's still a long way to go. But they are a very disciplined side who are very hard to break down and, apart from last week, they don't concede many goals. That always gives them a chance to win games. It's a very difficult game but it should be a big match and a great atmosphere, and these are the type of games you want to be involved in.'

And Sunderland had to dig deep into their resources to keep the promotion bandwagon on course at Oakwell. Craig Russell fired the Rokermen into a 23rd-minute lead with his 13th goal of the season, but Paul Stewart was sensationally sent off for violent conduct just before the half-time whistle to leave the gallant ten to fight a second-half rearguard action. But they were in no mood to surrender the three precious points and stretched an unbeaten run to 13 matches, even though goalkeeper Shay Given was badly shaken in the later stages. It was first feared he may have cracked ribs, and though X-rays failed to reveal any break, the injury proved serious enough to signal the end of his three-month stay and he returned to Blackburn Rovers a bitterly disappointed young man.

Alec Chamberlain took over for the Easter Monday afternoon visit against promotion rivals Charlton Athletic and the experienced keeper emerged with credit and proved in a goalless draw that he is there to answer the call in the club's hour of need:

It was nice to come into a side obviously going well and full of confidence, so that made it easier. The crowd was very good and gave me a great reception. It was like starting where I left off in many ways. It made me feel I must have done all right in the first half of the season, otherwise they would not have given me that sort of reception. It was a nice confidence booster and fortunately I kept a clean sheet.

I'm always nervous before a match, but I had butterflies this time. That shows you want to do well because if you are too laid back and relaxed about it, I don't think you can perform. Shay has done ever so well and if I had conceded goals and we had lost, I could have been to blame. Thankfully, it didn't go like that. Hopefully it is going to be a nice end of season for me and I will be in for the glory.

Peter Reid still preferred to look on the bright side and considered the result a point gained rather than two lost in the quest for promotion. He said: 'Charlton made it very difficult for us and, without making excuses, I thought we looked half a yard off it, possibly because of the 45 minutes we played with ten men at Barnsley. All in all I am delighted we didn't concede a goal against Charlton – they are not bad away from home. From the position we are in, if we keep clean sheets we will go up.'

Derby hammered Tranmere Rovers 6–2 and Crystal Palace won by two clear goals at Reading to close the gap and keep up the relentless pressure.

Top of the First Division after the Easter programme:

		P	W	D	L	F	A	Pts
1	Sunderland	41	21	14	6	56	31	77
2	Derby County	42	20	14	8	66	46	74
3	Crystal Palace	42	18	15	9	62	45	69
4	Charlton	40	16	16	8	53	42	64

7

We Are the Champions

Craig Russell returned to the attack for the visit to Sheffield United aiming to repeat his fairy-tale goalscoring exploits against the Blades. He hit the last-gasp winner to kick-start Peter Reid's successful battle against relegation a year previously, though the sides met in vastly different circumstances this time round with Sunderland defending an unbeaten 14-match run three points clear at the top and their opponents making a belated charge for the play-offs on the strength of five successive victories.

Said Craig Russell: 'It's amazing how the fortunes of both clubs have changed since we met a year ago. Ours is very much for the better while Sheffield, who were in turmoil not too long ago, could possibly sneak into the play-offs after a great run of results.

'I will never forget last season's game at Roker Park. It was the gaffer's first game in charge and I was on the bench. He chucked me on and asked me to get him a goal. I managed to do it and it really was an important one. It gave us a kick-start for survival and it would be lovely to do the same again, for a completely different reason.'

Goals were again at a premium at Bramall Lane, however, with a second successive goalless draw the outcome as Sunderland stretched the unbeaten run to 15 matches. Craig Russell, however, admitted he had had chances to move off the unlucky 13 tally for the season: 'I am disappointed not to have scored, but I would be more concerned if I was not getting into positions to miss. The pitch was very bobbly and it was a hard surface to play on – and that's not making excuses.'

United coach and right-hand man to Howard Kendall at Bramall Lane, former Sunderland assistant manager Viv Busby, had no doubts Sunderland's promotion dream would be realised in the near future: 'I would not bet against them and, if they beat Birmingham City tomorrow night, they will have a foot in the door. They defend well and Alec Chamberlain showed what a good pro he is. It's good to see him back and you can't knock him.' Peter Reid still refused to set targets in the big countdown to promotion, but acknowledged a four-match unbeaten run would do the trick: 'It's in our own hands over the last four games. We've gone 15 games unbeaten – I can't ask for any more. We've gone out there, we've worked hard, and we've earned what we've got. That's pleasing for me. Both sides had a couple of chances and, in the end, I think a draw was a fair result.'

Derby County manager Jim Smith believed his side's scrambled goalless draw with Charlton Athletic effectively knocked the Londoners out of the race for automatic promotion. In theory, Charlton, whose challenge had been a triumph of will over the flimsiest resources, could overtake both Derby and Sunderland. But they were ten points adrift of the former and a further three points behind Peter Reid's side with five to play. Said Jim Smith: 'I think that effectively we've knocked them out of the race. But I never really saw them as contenders. It'll be between the three of us. Two of Crystal Palace's last three games are away and one of them's against us. If we get four points out of the next two home games, we'll be up, it's as simple as that.' Dave Bassett acknowledged his side were the outsiders of the three-horse race even though they strolled to a two-goal win at Southend. He said: 'I'd rather be in Sunderland or Derby County's position than ours. We can only win our games, we can't do any more. In a sense, unless Sunderland or Derby slip up, it's immaterial. All we can say is that we are in third place on merit.'

Top of the First Division on 14 April:

		P	W	D	L	F	A	Pts
1	Sunderland	42	21	15	6	56	31	78
2	Derby County	43	20	15	8	66	46	75
3	Crystal Palace	43	19	15	9	64	45	72
4	Charlton	41	16	17	8	53	42	65

With the Premiership beckoning, cash for team strengthening became even more essential with speculation of a possible stock market flotation appearing in the *Financial Times*. Club officials, however, were quick to say it was only one option and 'it was by no means a major consideration'. A senior executive at the club said: 'The whole financing of the club is being looked at in great detail at the moment . . . and a flotation is being considered as an option.'

Paul Stewart's dismissal at Barnsley ruled the former England international out of the last three games of the season and he went into the rearranged home game against Birmingham City desperate to sign off with a goal – and on a winning note:

> I want to go out with a bang. Nothing is finalised about a contract yet, so this could be my last game for Sunderland. The manager has talked about offering me a contract but when I was at Crystal Palace on loan they were sitting down and offering me a contract, and it was the same at Wolves and I ended up with nothing. I don't want to tempt fate but I am pleased the manager has said he is going to offer me a contract. I would love to sign, there is no doubt in my mind. I have enjoyed it here but I would have liked to have scored a couple of goals. I know I have set a few up but strikers are judged and remembered for the number of goals they score.

The sending-off at Oakwell upset Stewart bitterly, and while he acknowledged he made contact with his opponent, there was no intent: 'I'm disappointed because there was no malice in what happened. The lad has pulled me down and as we were going along, I have just tried to get up. The ref had not blown for a foul and then the lad started screaming. It was a game where there was no need for anything like that and he hadn't clouted me. I was on the floor and just tried to brush him off. I was disappointed in how the ref interpreted things.'

Birmingham manager Barry Fry was in the mood to throw a spanner in the works and make amends for the defeat on home soil just a few weeks earlier. He said: 'I felt humiliated. Sunderland walked all over us, so I want to go up there and give them the fright of their lives.' Two goals in the opening 21 minutes scuppered that theory and the Birmingham manager was again reduced to singing the praises of a Sunderland side needing a single point from three matches to be mathematically certain of winning promotion. A stunning 30-yard volley from Michael Gray in the 18th minute was followed three minutes later by a Paul Stewart header, and on 62 minutes Craig Russell made sure Sunderland equalled a 73-year-old record of 16 games unbeaten. Fry switched to a five-man defence for the first time in his two and a half years as manager of the Blues, but switched to a normal back-four line-up for the second-half when sending on all three substitutes: 'If I had all my 43 players out there I don't think it would have worked. Sunderland are a good side, as I've said before. 'They showed us up at home, humiliating us, and they did the same again. They're just too good for us, too strong, too aggressive, too clever and wanted it more. They'll go up as champions. When they came to our place I said they would win it by ten points and we are a million miles behind them. Peter Reid has done a marvellous job and Paul Stewart is a tremendous free signing – if you forget his 28 grand a week!'

An elated Paul Stewart signed off in style and deservedly picked up the man-of-the-match award. He said: 'It's a long time since my last goal, I think it was for Wolves against Tranmere, but I got injured and was out for three months, so it was not such a happy occasion. That was my last game of the season and I wanted to go out on a high note. If I hadn't I would have mulled over the close season. I can't wait for next season.' Peter Reid finally released his emotions after guiding the club from the depths of despair to almost crossing the finishing line in the promotion stakes:

I can't put into words the difference from a year ago. I am bursting with pride. What we have achieved in the last twelve months gives me more satisfaction than anything I ever achieved as a player. I have played at Wembley, but, if we are promoted at the weekend, that will be my best day in football, without a doubt. I have enjoyed the season and last night I thought the players looked as though they enjoy playing at Roker Park. That gives me a big buzz.

I will be disappointed if we don't go up now. I just want to be mathematically certain before any celebration. All I will say is the white wine is out in the office and the champagne will have to keep on ice. But that was a performance of a side that looks as though it is going up. There wasn't a bad player out there.

Sometimes, as a manager, you wonder whether they can handle the pressures. I just thought we were very positive and I didn't see anxiety in the players. At a football club, you get into habits and keep going. I was looking at the players in the last five minutes and they were encouraging each other. That's tremendous.

Top of the First Division on 16 April:

		P	W	D	L	F	A	Pts
1	Sunderland	43	22	15	6	59	31	81
2	Derby County	43	20	15	8	66	46	75
3	Crystal Palace	43	19	15	9	64	45	72
4	Charlton	41	16	17	8	53	42	65
5	Stoke City	41	17	12	12	55	45	63

Stoke City, desperate for points to sustain a top-six challenge, and the only side in a position to complete the double over Sunderland, were also to prove durable opponents before the live television cameras. But there was always the chance Sunderland's destiny could be decided the previous afternoon. For Crystal Palace to win the First Division Championship, they had to win all three remaining games, starting with a tough visit to Wolves, and Sunderland lose all three. The equation was further complicated by Palace's visit to Derby a week later. If Derby failed to win their home game with Birmingham City it would mean both Jim Smith's side and Palace couldn't match Sunderland's current number of points.

Peter Reid decided against travelling to either venue and instead made the short trip down the M1 motorway to watch another crucial promotion match from the Third Division: 'I will be at Darlington watching Bury. I will be hoping that two great friends of mine, Stan Ternant and Sam Ellis, get a good result for Bury. I just think that someone at Darlington might mention to me that we are up if that proves to be the case. I find it hard to watch Teletext for the results or listen to Radio Five. I will just watch the Darlington-Bury game.' Darlington thrashed Bury 4–0 to move into a play-off position to take the shine off the trip to Feethams and leave Reid's pals to sweat on their own promotion prospects. But when news filtered through that Birmingham had surprisingly held Derby County to a draw at the Baseball Ground, the party celebrations were underway. Said Peter Reid:

> A year ago I don't think anybody in their right minds would look a year on and see Sunderland Football Club in this position. I thought we would go near to the play-offs. We have to be realistic because we have done it without Martin Smith, David Kelly and Phil Gray for a fair bit of the season. I am delighted the way the season has gone and all I say to everybody connected with the club is enjoy it and don't even think about the Premiership. I will sort that out in the summer; just enjoy what we have done. This is a big club and the supporters, who have been brilliant, deserve the success we can now enjoy.

And looking ahead to the game against Stoke City in the chase of a club record of 17 unbeaten games, Reid added:

> We've been in a limbo situtation for the last few days just waiting for confirmation that we have done it. But it's not all about what has happened today. It comes down to the fact we have lost six games out of forty-three. That's the reason why we are top, not because of what anybody else has done. We are on a run since Lee Howey's late equaliser at Portsmouth and I can't stress how important that goal was. I want to thank everybody, especially the players who have been magnificent. I am the front man but Paul Bracewell and Bobby Saxton have done tremendously well behind the scenes.

Promotion guaranteed, Sunderland needed victory against Stoke City to clinch the First Division Championship. Lee Howey came in for the suspended Paul Stewart to add height and weight to the attack but Sunderland were far from their Sunday best against a dour Stoke side more than content to settle for a point from a goalless draw to enhance their own promotion prospects. The game, beamed out live to six regional stations, gave cynics claiming Sunderland will struggle in the Premiership next season a field day. Large sections of the bumper crowd had drifted away before the referee decided it was time to bring the stalemate to a close.

Top of the First Division on 21 April:

		P	W	D	L	F	A	Pts
1	Sunderland	44	22	16	6	59	31	82
2	Derby County	44	20	16	8	67	47	76
3	Crystal Palace	44	20	15	9	66	45	75
4	Stoke City	43	18	13	12	56	45	67
5	Charlton	43	16	18	9	53	43	66

There was no let-up in the quest for the First Division Championship. The celebrations may have been in full swing and the manager consuming his fair share of the champagne, but he remained single-minded: 'Let's just enjoy the rest of this season. The job is not yet complete and will only be so after we have played the last game at Tranmere. Until then, I won't even be thinking about next season. One more point will do us. I could sense the lads were desperate to get a victory but we didn't get it. The fact we made it 17 games unbeaten, speaks for itself. It will be a special occasion when we do get the point and I will take this year, compared to last, any day.'

The changing room after the Stoke game was a chaotic mixture of champagne and sing-song chants. Reid was drenched from head to toe by his cock-a-hoop players, but he didn't mind a bit. Skipper Kevin Ball said: 'I'm sorry about you getting drenched gaffer. I think it was Scotty – shall I fine him a week's wages?'

Ex-Poland international Dariusz Kubicki talked of the team spirit and respect for the management team. He said: 'These players would die for each other. The team spirit has been fantastic. I'm delighted for them. Everyone at the club has done something in this season.' His full-back partner Martin Scott said: 'A long, hard season, but we deserve what we've got. It's been a great team effort from day one. The gaffer has been different class and gets the best out of every player and the lads love playing for him.' Gareth Hall, though forced to take a back seat on the substitutes bench for long spells after his mid-season move from Chelsea, said: 'I've loved it.

It's been magnificent. Sunderland are the best team in the League and deserve to go up as champions.' Former England Under-21 international Richard Ord could not have dreamed of celebrating his testimonial season with a championship medal. 'This is the best ever,' he said. 'It's tremendous.' His partner at the heart of the defence, Andy Melville, chipped in: 'What can I say. We've done it and we're up.'

Local lad and former British Telecom engineer Lee Howey was more pleased with the result than the performance. 'It was a scrappy game. We always knew it was going to be tough and Stoke did well to stop us playing. But at the end of the day, the important thing is that we are up and we have another point towards the championship.' And Michael Bridges, the baby of the pack, still months away from even being able to buy a pint in a pub, consoled himself for missing the chance which would have guaranteed the title: 'I'm still gutted about missing that chance when I only had the goalkeeper to beat. But I can't complain too much can I, really. Last season, I was collecting schoolboy medals, this season I'm collecting an Endsleigh League First Division medal.' Fellow teenager Sam Aiston, who also came off the substitutes bench in a last throw of the dice to snatch the winner, was also in buoyant mood: 'I'm still choked about missing the good chance I had, but I guess I will settle for a championship medal in my first season as a professional footballer.'

Bob Murray wasted no time in contacting leading Premiership officials to determine the extent of the club's new-found status, though a point was still needed from two remaining games before the Championship flag would be flying over Roker Park next season:

I have already been in contact with the Premiership at the highest level. I was on the phone on Monday morning, the soonest possible after promotion was confirmed. Everything is different between the Premiership and the Football League. We are talking about the way it is managed because it's run like a consortium. We need to get up to speed with it very quickly. Commercial deals are happening now that we have no knowledge of. The board is not up to speed to talk about Peter Reid's personal terms or about money for players coming in. Peter has one year of his contract to run and we have several players out of contract. The board must be responsible. The top priority is the team and Peter Reid and we have thrown ourselves into it. We know we have some excellent players at the club, but it's taken Peter's excellent managerial ability to bring it out.

With skipper Kevin Ball suspended for the home game with West Brom, Gareth Hall was given a rare chance in central midfield. The Welsh international had been forced to be content with a place on the substitutes bench for all but six of the games since his mid-season move from Chelsea.

It's been a long wait, but not unexpected. I got into the side but did not really expect to stay there. After all, the lads in the team were the ones who got us to the top of the League. I couldn't really expect to come in and take a shirt off the back of a couple of games.

It's a great game though to come back for. I played in the game which won Chelsea the Second Division Championship in 1989. I think we went up with 98 points and absolutely stormed it that year when Graham Roberts and Peter Nicholas were in the side. They did it in style and it would be nice to do it again with Sunderland and go out in a blaze of glory. It's nice just to be getting a game and if I do well, who knows what will happen next season. I would expect Kevin Ball to come back for the last match of the season at Tranmere, after all he is the captain, but I am sure the gaffer will give everybody involved a run out.

West Brom got the season off to a flying start but the worst run of results in the club's history plunged Alan Buckley's side into the relegation zone. Nevertheless, a return to the early-season form lifted Brom into a comfortable mid-table position and set the scene for a carnival Roker Park atmosphere. The celebrations started long before the kick-off but the fans had to be content to endure a second successive goalless home draw on the way to clinching the First Division Championship. Sunderland had the game by the scruff of the neck but were again unable to turn their superiority into goals.

Derby County, too, were in the party mood after clinching the other automatic promotion spot at the expense of bitter rivals Crystal Palace. A 2–1 home win over Dave Bassett's side confirmed a return to the top flight, five years after they were relegated alongside Sunderland. Chairman Lionel Pickering had sunk £12 million into Derby since taking control in 1991, but admitted there would not be unlimited funds to spend on team strengthening. Derby are building a brand-new 30,000 all-seater stadium, and Pickering admitted: 'We have the problem of staying in the Premiership and building a new stadium. The team must be our priority, although we cannot afford a lot of cash as we must meet the demands on the stadium.'

Top of the First Division on 28 April:

		P	W	D	L	F	A	Pts
1	Sunderland	45	22	17	6	59	31	83
2	Derby County	45	21	16	8	69	48	79
3	Crystal Palace	45	20	15	10	67	47	75
4	Stoke City	44	19	13	12	59	47	70
5	Charlton	44	17	18	9	56	44	69
6	Leicester City	45	18	14	13	65	60	68

The championship in the bag, a shattered Paul Bracewell decided to opt out of the final game of the season against Tranmere Rovers and take a well-earned rest in the dug-out along with the rest of the management team: 'I talked it over with the gaffer and we decided as soon as we had won the championship, I would call it a day for the season. If we had beaten Stoke City, I would not have played against West Bromwich. I am absolutely shattered. This will give one of the other lads the chance of a game and I will enjoy being on the bench with the manager.'

Gareth Hall therefore was given an unexpected reprieve to accommodate the return of Kevin Ball, but Andy Melville picked up an overnight virus. Lee Howey switched to central defence and Michael Bridges came into the attack for only his second start. Not even a 2–0 defeat after 18 unbeaten matches was ever going to spoil Sunderland's farewell from the Endsleigh League. The fans travelled in their thousands to Tranmere to celebrate promotion to the Premiership. And, if only a couple of the bucketful of chances had been accepted, an end to the best-ever unbeaten run in the club's history would have been averted. Tranmere, completely outplayed in the first-half, took full advantage to extend John Aldridge's player-manager start to six unbeaten games and maintain a 100 per cent record from the only five meetings between the clubs at Prenton Park. A first-half header from Kenny Irons and a dubious John Aldridge penalty gave the home side victory. Martin Scott, who conceded the penalty, quickly raised deflated spirits.

> We are just disappointed that we haven't been able to give the fans the win they wanted. They have been fantastic all season and when one of them asked me for my shirt as we did the lap of honour, it was the least I could do.
>
> I've got my red-and-white one and I will cherish that for a very long time. At least one fan went home happy. It's just as well we didn't need a result, but we finished top of the League and, as far as I am concerned, we have proved we are the best over 46 games. The dressing-room was a bit flat when the gaffer came in and reminded us we are the champions. We felt a bit better after that.

Andy Melville set his sights on a return to the international scene to compensate for the disappointment of missing out on another party crowned by a lap of honour to the delight of the supporters of both clubs. He was banking on the best season of his career for a recall to the Wales squad for the start of the World Cup qualification programme against San Marino:

> There was a bit of a bug going around and I was sick on Sunday morning. I wanted to play and keep the run going but I was ill again just before the start and there is no way I could have played. But we've had a brilliant season and it has worked out well for me. I wasn't in the side at the start and it looked as though I might have a long wait. Dickie Ord got injured at Preston in the Coca-Cola Cup and, apart from suspension, I've only missed one other game. For the last six seasons I've been involved in relegation battles with the last match nearly always proving crucial.
>
> To win promotion with three games to go was a new experience and the icing on the cake would be a recall to the Wales squad. I lost my place in the squad because of club commitments, then I wasn't in the squad for the next match. I had to drop out of a get-together

because of injury and that again seems to have cost me my place.

The last day of the campaign proved disappointing for the top three clubs, Derby losing 3–2 at West Brom and Crystal Palace, already guaranteed third spot, losing 1–0 at home to Norwich City.

Top of the First Division at end of season:

		P	W	D	L	F	A	Pts
1	Sunderland	46	22	17	7	59	33	83
2	Derby County	46	21	16	9	71	51	79
3	Crystal Palace	46	20	15	11	67	48	75
4	Stoke City	46	20	13	13	60	49	73
5	Leicester City	46	19	14	13	66	60	71
6	Charlton	46	17	20	9	57	45	71

Sunderland and Derby County were promoted automatically, and Leicester City via the play-offs. Leicester beat Stoke City over two legs and Crystal Palace squeezed out Charlton Athletic. Steve Claridge hit a last-gasp extra-time winner for Leicester in the Bank Holiday play-off final at Wembley.

8

Goalkeepers

The two goalkeepers who helped Sunderland shatter a club record of 21 clean sheets in a season accepted they would not be in direct opposition again for the coveted jersey. Alec Chamberlain was forced to live under the shadow of a replacement coming in at any time, and while he finished the season between the posts and has been offered a new contract, he was transferred to Watford for a fee of £40,000.

He played in the first 29 games of the championship season and returned for the last six matches when Shay Given returned to Blackburn Rovers. Chamberlain found it hard to bear when Peter Reid turned to an unknown 19-year-old for a month on loan midway through the campaign.

Given, however, after a nervous début in a goalless draw against Leicester City at Filbert Street, quickly became a cult hero with the supporters. No opposition could find a way past the confident young Irishman from Donegal in seven successive home games before he was finally beaten by Huddersfield Town's Rob Edwards. His loan spell was extended to the three-month maximum and his outstanding displays won him a first full Republic of Ireland cap against Russia. Reid went to great lengths to have the teenager available for an extra game by delaying the third month's loan period, but to no avail. Given was badly shaken in a 1–0 win at Barnsley, and though X-rays confirmed no ribs had been broken, his magnificent achievement of

12 shut-outs in 17 games was brought to a premature end. With the transfer deadline expired, Chamberlain was back in business.

And how the 32-year-old responded and grabbed his belated chance with both hands to give the manager food for thought of a new contract by keeping five successive clean sheets on his return:

> There was no jealousy on my part. Obviously I was disappointed to be dropped, but goalkeepers support each other and I wish Shay all the best in the world. I will be delighted for him if he keeps more clean sheets and goes on to become the Republic of Ireland's first-choice goalkeeper for years.
>
> It all made for a cracking end of season. It was important for me, with the team doing so well and in a promotion position, to come in and play my part again. I played the first half of the season and to come in, play the last six games and finish with a medal, has exceeded my wildest dreams. It's been nice to play my part and, with Shay being such a cult hero, I didn't know what sort of reception to expect from the fans. The supporters have been brilliant and hopefully we can take this into the Premiership. We have to roll our sleeves up and start all over again.

Supporters were so impressed with Given's performances a fund was launched to raise cash for Peter Reid to try and sign Blackburn's third-choice goalkeeper on a permanent basis. The stumbling block was not cash: Rovers were simply not interested in parting with one of the best young keepers in the business. Said Given:

> The supporters have been great. I was disappointed when I had to go back to Blackburn, but there was nothing I could do about it. It's just one of those things. I enjoyed the chance to play first-team football and there's a big difference between Blackburn's third team in the Lancashire League and crowds of 21,000 at Roker Park. Playing first-team football helps me to be a better goalkeeper and has enhanced my international prospects.
>
> A First Division Championship medal, however, is a wonderful souvenir. I was with the Premiership Champions last season and, though I didn't play, I was involved. It is a wonderful double being with the First Division Champions this season. That's some double.

Peter Reid predicts a bright future for Given, who has been given the chance to challenge England international Tim Flowers for the goalkeeper's jersey on the release of Bobby Mimms on a free transfer: 'He's got great hands. He's the best young goalkeeper that I have seen. Ray Harford, the Blackburn manager, thinks very highly of him so there's no chance of us signing him. Unfortunately, that's the way it is and I doubt very much whether it will change. But Shay has played his part.'

On the eve of flying out to America in the close season to represent the Republic of Ireland in the US Cup with matches against the United States, Mexico and Bolivia, Given made a startling 'come and get me plea' to Reid. He had made five successive appearances for the Irish after replacing the injured Alan Kelly and realised his best chance of further international honours was a regular first-team place:

> I know Peter Reid is keen to buy me and I'm very flattered. It's obviously my ambition to play regularly at the very top and coming into the Ireland team for such a testing run of games this year has helped me a great deal. I'm learning a lot from Celtic's Packie Bonner, the Irish goalkeeping coach. At Blackburn my chances are limited, although they've given Bobby Mimms a free transfer and I'm the No. 2 keeper now, I still have Tim Flowers in front of me. I really enjoyed my time at Sunderland last season and I'm waiting to see if Peter Reid comes in again for me.

Reid failed in an attempt to sign Hearts goalkeeper Gilles Rousset. He confirmed he had made an inquiry for the 6ft 7in French international and was reported to have offered strikers Lee Howey and Brett Angell in exchange for the £500,000-rated goalkeeper. Rousset was snapped up by Hearts on a free transfer and made such a favourable impression that manager Jim Jefferies signed him up on a four-year contract: 'When I found out that Gilles was available on a free transfer, I thought he must have an arm missing. He's one of the best goalkeepers I have seen. Andy Goram and Jim Leighton are our big two in Scotland and Gilles is up there with them. The fact he has been on the substitutes bench 28 times for France and played twice for them – once against England at Wembley – speaks for itself.'

Reid was also close to signing Manchester City goalkeeper Tony Coton, and a cut-price fee of £400,000 was agreed with City manager Alan Ball. But Coton surprisingly opted to move across the City of Manchester and sign for Alex Ferguson as cover for Peter Schmeichel.

Sunderland conceded just 33 goals in 46 League games and Alec Chamberlain and Shay Given kept a total of 25 clean sheets between them. Only two teams, Ipswich Town and Wolves, scored more than twice in any one game and neither managed to find the net at Roker Park. And though Kevin Ball hailed the performances of the two goalkeepers and the back four players, he insists the key to success of the meanest defensive record in the division was due to team work and not individuals. Until recently, Kevin Ball made no secret of the fact his favourite position was in central defence, but his switch to a central midfield role has been a revelation:

As a defender or defensive-minded midfielder, the first thing I look for is the goals-against column, and to be fair ours has always been pretty good. Defensively we have been superb all season but as I have always said, attacking and scoring goals is a team effort and the same goes for defenders.

When we do our tactical work on Thursdays and Fridays before a game, we spend a lot of time on how we will attack and how we will defend. It's always done as a team game. The back five have been superb throughout and only on the rare occasion have we taken a battering. Defensively we could not have asked for any more from the two goalkeepers. Alec has been first-class and then Shay came in and did very well. The two full-backs, Dariusz and Scottie, not only defend well, but get forward as much as possible which is important. The two centre-backs, Ordie and Mel, have complemented each other as the season has gone on, and apart from the odd game or two when they were suspended, they have been together nearly all season. At the end of the day we are top of the League and there is a saying the best team finishes top. The back five have done tremendously well but we defend and attack as a unit and that's why we finished where we did.

9

Record Breakers

Sunderland entered the *Guinness Book of Hit Records*, and would have been the leading contender for 'chant of the year award'. The terrace anthem of 'Cheer Up Peter Reid' reached number 49 in the national charts on the first week of release. Next week it reached 41 in the charts, prompting talk of a possible *Top of the Pops* appearance. The record peaked at 41, but it had still gone high enough to warrant inclusion in the *Guinness Book of Hit Records* which notes all singles which get higher than number 75.

Seven fans recorded the chant 'Cheer Up Peter Reid, oh what can it mean to a Sunderland supporter, when you are top of the League' to the tune of the Monkees' 'Daydream Believer'. It stemmed from Reid's almost obsessive desire not to unfairly raise the hopes of the fans, his dead-pan chewing-gum face giving nothing away as he leaned on the dug-out. Diehards claim the chant was first taken up at Fratton Park when Lee Howey's last-gasp equaliser set the ball rolling towards an unbeaten 18-match run. The London Branch of the Sunderland Supporters' Association stalwarts Jim Minton and Steve Trow were having a night out in the Windmill, Clapham Common, when they heard a local band playing the Monkees' hit.

Together they thought up the words, but the record really came into its own in the 4–0 thrashing at Grimsby and the track quickly caught the imagination of the public; pictures of the new pop stars appeared in virtually every newspaper in the country. Television took an interest and the song was featured on BBC's *Look North*, ITV's Endsleigh League round-up and Channel 4's *Big Breakfast*. It even made an appearance in poster form behind Statto on *Fantasy Football League*.

Sunderland fans are renowned for their humour and they certainly put the smile on the faces of football supporters worldwide for their rendering of Roker's National Anthem.

DAYDREAM BELIEVER (Cheer Up Peter Reid)

Oh I could fly without wings
On the back of Reidy's kings,
At three o'clock I'm happy as can be;
Cos the good times they are here
And the Premiership is near,
So watch out world as all of Roker sings.

Chorus

Cheer up Peter Reid,
Oh what can it mean
To a Sunderland supporter
To be top of the League,
We once thought of you
As a Scouser dressed in blue,
Now you're red and white and Sunderland through.
We had all dreamed of the day
When a saviour would come our way,
And now we know our dreams are coming true

Chorus

The track sold more copies in Sunderland's HMV store than Oasis's 'Look'. It reached number one in NME's Indie chart, and had the record only been sold in recognised retail outlets it would have reached the top 20. The track was the brainchild of Andy Forsyth, who masterminded the record after Ian Chester, Gary Raine, Martyn McFadden, Tom Lynn, Sean Vasey, Steve Atkinson and Paul Davison provided the vocals. The song has raised thousands of pounds for charity including £2,000 for Reid's own charity, the Malcolm Sargent Children's Cancer Fund.

Sunderland were record-breakers on other fronts, too, with club records for consecutive wins, unbeaten runs, home goals conceded and the number of clean sheets all surpassed during a remarkable campaign. The record of nine successive victories started against Ipswich and continued through to the 3–3 draw at Watford, during which time only three goals were conceded. The previous record was established in the Championship-winning season of 1891/92 when 13 games were won on the trot, a 1–0 defeat at Notts County the only blemish in a 17-game finish to the season. The run of 17 unbeaten games, ended on the final day of the season at Tranmere, beat the previous best of 16 established in 1922 and equalled the final 14 games of 1979/80 and the opening two of the following season. A 2–0 home win over Newcastle United on 11 November 1922 running through to a 3–1 defeat at Sheffield United four months later contributed to Sunderland finishing the season second to Liverpool.

Only ten goals were conceded at Roker Park which easily beat the previous best of 22 for a 46-game season, established in the Third Division Championship season of 1987/88. Ten home goals were leaked on the way to the promotion season of 1975/76, but only 42 games were played, two fewer at home and away.

The clean sheet record of 26 set by Shay Given (12) and Alec Chamberlain (14) easily shattered the previous best of 21 in 1974/75. Then, Trevor Swinburne kept out the Manchester United attack in a goalless draw at Roker Park with Jimmy Montgomery keeping goal for the other 20 blanks.

Chapters of Sunderland's history have been marked by the changing colour of the local evening newspaper's popular *Football Echo*, published on Saturday nights throughout the season. The first change was made towards the end of the 1912/13 season, when supplies of pink paper were unobtainable, and the first edition to be printed on white paper appeared on the night of Sunderland's defeat by Aston Villa in the FA Cup Final at Crystal Palace. After the First World War the *Football Echo* was printed on blue paper and there were repeated requests from readers that it should revert to pink. A promise was made that success in the Cup would bring the change. The day came in 1937, when the Roker team beat Preston at Wembley.

The story continues with white then blue following relegation on 26 April 1958, and a return to pink with promotion on 18 April 1964. With relegation on 15 April 1970, the *Football Echo* went blue again but the flush of a FA Cup final victory over Leeds United on 5 May 1973, saw the the return of the 'Pink 'un' to mark a memorable occasion. It remained pink until the brave fight against relegation ended with a 2–0 defeat at Everton on 19 May 1977, turning white with shock two days later. For the start of the 1977/78 season, the Football Echo reverted to pink.

Sunderland's list of honours includes six Championship wins in 1891/92 (when all 13 home games were won), 1892/93 (100 goals were scored from 30 games), 1894/95 (unbeaten at home), 1901/02, 1912/13 (went from bottom to top after only two points from the first seven games) and 1935/36 (scored 109 goals). Runners-up in 1893/94, 1897/98, 1900/01, 1922/23, 1934/35. Second Division Champions 1975/76; runners-up 1963/64, 1979/80. Third Division Champions 1987/88. FA Cup winners 1937 and 1973; runners-up 1913 and 1992. Milk Cup finalists 1985.

Other statistics of note include: Most appearances: 623 Jimmy Montgomery, 456 Teddy Doig, 452 Len Ashurst, 447 Stan Anderson, 428 Gary Bennett, 413 Charlie Buchan and Bobby Kerr, 400 Charlie Hurley. Leading goalscorer: 228 Bobby Gurney, 224 Charlie Buchan, 162 Dave Halliday, 154 George Holley, 150 Johnny Campbell, 130 Raich Carter, 123 Jimmy Millar, 118 Arthur Bridgett, 108 Patsy Gallacher, 101 Len Shackleton, 98 Gary Rowell.

10

Reid and Staff

The speed of taking Sunderland out of the First Division and into the Premiership took even Peter Reid by surprise. Sunderland were transformed from no-hopers struggling to avoid relegation into First Division champions in just over twelve months. Sacked by Manchester City after two finishes of fifth and a season in ninth place, the durable Scouser bounced back to become the darling of Wearside:

I have always had confidence in my own ability in football. I had my knocks as a young player, including a contract dispute and a serious injury, but these things are sent to try us. You have just got to get up and get in there again. Even though I was confident, I must admit I am back in the Premiership a bit quicker than I thought it would take. I just thought with a bit of luck we would get into the play-offs. But everything has gone superbly well and we've lost seven League games in 52. That's brilliant and speaks volumes for the spirit here.

In football you make decisions and I am delighted that I made the right one. I turned down four or five jobs during the 18 months I was out of management. That's an awful long time. Other people took jobs for the sake of it and it has gone the other way. So even though I was asked to take the Sunderland job in the position they were in, I jumped at it and I was delighted. I knew it was right and it was the job I had been waiting for. There was only a handful of clubs and I was waiting for the right one. I have always had ties with Roker. I had been out for a year when I snapped my cruciate ligament and my first game back was an FA Cup-tie at Roker Park which Bolton won 1–0.

And he was manager of Manchester City when Sunderland, with just an outside chance of staving off relegation in the final game of the 1990/91 season, took 15,000 fans to Maine Road. 'I remember Denis Smith being very emotional in the tunnel afterwards,' said Reid. 'The Sunderland fans were absolutely first-class and I was amazed at the scenes in the ground before, during and after the match.

Manchester City is a big club and the crowd is vociferous but I've never seen or heard anything like that. When Marco Gabbiadini scored the stadium was just red and white – that's a Sunderland supporter for you. Those things stick in your mind.'

But while the buck stops at the manager's door, Reid is only too pleased for the rest of the backroom staff to join in the plaudits. Assistant manager Paul Bracewell, coach Bobby Saxton, reserve team coach Pop Robson, youth team coach Ricky Sbragia and chief scout Alan Durban all made vital contributions in revamping the club for the future: 'Our success is down to the players and the backroom staff. They have been brilliant and I am delighted for everybody at the club. The players have worked extremely hard and I could not have asked for any more.'

The renowned Roker Roar took to the road and played no small part in the success with Reid, his management team and players acknowledging the magnificent support throughout the season. And recognition of the achievement was not confined to Sunderland supporters as Reid recalls:

The amount I received was staggering. I never knew there were so many Sunderland supporters all over the world. It's amazing. Jim Smith was straight on the phone after we won promotion and I thought that was brilliant considering Derby County still had it all to do. For a manager to take time off like that when he had a crunch game coming up with Crystal Palace was brilliant. I had a smashing letter from Trevor Hartley (the sacked coach). Full credit to the man but I just felt I had to bring my own people in.

People keep telling me what a rubbish division this is, how rubbish it was last season and the year before. I just can't agree. There are some good sides in this League and you only have to look at some of this season's Cup results to see that. I don't think anybody in their right minds would look a year on and see Sunderland Football Club where they are. Realistically, I thought we could reach the play-offs.'

And having marched into the Premiership as champions, Reid will not be content with just survival among the big boys:

I think, if you go into a league, you have got to have a chance of trying to do well. I just want to try to build a football team that the fans can relate to in what I think is the best league in the world.

It's going to be difficult, but people didn't think we would do it this year – me among them! It's up to us to improve it and if quality players become available, Sunderland Football Club should be in there for them and hopefully I will be. I think we will be able to compete for the best players and, if you get the best players, you have got a chance.

I was certainly low after the Manchester City sacking, but these things happen in football. Managers getting the sack is all part and parcel of football and you always have your lows.

He was certainly on a high though – and mentally drained – when he watched his side presented with the First Division Championship trophy. He beckoned his 13-year-old daughter Louise to join him from the terraces in the lap of honour.

In *Paul Bracewell*, the Roker manager found the perfect partner to lead Sunderland back into the big time. The £50,000 handed over to Newcastle United for him must be considered one of the bargains of all time. Bracewell was a major influence throughout the promotion campaign, with not even a mid-season groin operation – the 14th of his career – preventing him from playing his part both on and off the field. Views differed greatly on the turning point of the season, with Bracewell citing the return leg of the first round of the Coca-Cola Cup with Preston a morale-boosting victory.

The gaffer thinks Lee Howey's late equaliser at Portsmouth was very important as it set us on our way to an unbeaten 18-match run and Bobby Saxton said if we had lost to Wolves we would have had only one point on the board from our first three games. But I think the turning point was the home game with Preston. We had already lost at home to Leicester City on the first day of the season and we were losing 2–0 at half-time of the Cup-tie. Then, all of a sudden, we pulled the game out of the fire and it just gave the lads belief to go on from there.

At the start of the season, we all sat down and decided how we wanted to play. The lads worked very hard at it, we were well organised and the team spirit was good. Another factor is they all now enjoy playing at Roker Park, which is very important. Prior to us coming, we could sense they did not like playing here. There had been two or three seasons of struggle where things had not gone well and we stressed that, to be successful, we had to win our home games. We only lost two and one of those was on the first day of the season. Ipswich were the only team to give us any problems, but we outplayed them down there and lost, so it evened itself out. At the end of the season, after 46 League games, the League table does not lie.

Some games you are not going to play particularly well and get results from, and in others you will play well and get beat. But overall I think we deserved to go up as champions. People said it was not a good League, but I think it has been a hard League and the most pleasing thing for me is the way the lads went about the job. I think they enjoyed going into work, enjoyed the training and believed in what they were trying to do. They enjoyed playing and I should imagine they have enjoyed the season. You can be the greatest trainers in the world, but if you don't get results on a Saturday afternoon, after a time it becomes different.

When I came here again I left a Premiership club and the aim, with the gaffer, was to get the club into the Premiership. We've done that and it's a great feeling. Our pre-season preparations went very well; that was the foundation of our success. We had four or five weeks when we could sit down together and plan what we were going to do. It was a question of getting our point across on how we wanted to do things.

The cynics predict Sunderland will be straight back down unless there is a dramatic cash injection ploughed into team strengthening, but Bracewell believes the four epic Cup-ties with Liverpool and Manchester United proved they will not be out of their depth:

> Winning is a great habit, and going up being able to look back on a great run of 18 unbeaten games will set us up nicely for next season. We didn't change our style against two of the best sides in the Premiership, Liverpool and Manchester United. And Manchester United paid us the compliment of changing their style when they came to Roker Park for the FA Cup replay. They didn't do that against many teams in the Premiership.
>
> I believe the basics will be the same next season: you stick to the things which have made you successful. A lot of things we did last season and a lot of things we instilled into the players will stand us in good stead in the Premiership. It's quite easy to have a couple of bad results and then push the panic button. We kept clean sheets and defended well, but we are not a defensive side. Very rarely do we play offside but you look at the record books and people might think that we are a boring side to watch. But that's not the case. We attack as a team and defend as a team. The lads can hardly wait to show what they can do in the Premiership – there's a buzz of anticipation about the club.

That was a far cry from when *Bobby Saxton* watched Peter Reid's rescue mission the previous season with more than just a passing interest. Saxton kept his distance but came to the decision shortly after the first phase had been successfully completed that he would accept the offer of first-team coach. He insists members of the coaching staff must gain the respect of the players on the training pitch as quickly as possible:

> When you first come to a club you don't know any of the players personally, though you may have heard of them. You may not like them, but you must respect them from a professional point of view and gain respect from them. But I can honestly say the players have been a pleasure to work with. It's important for everybody to go about their business in a professional manner. I get a tremendous

amount of self-satisfaction from the job and to win the First Division Championship is the Utopia. It's bringing the bacon home and we have climbed to the top of the mountain. Bearing in mind the situation – I had five years up the road at Newcastle – for it to happen as quickly as this is unbelievable.

Saxton, however, soon realised that far from facing another relegation struggle, the side had the potential to become a force to be reckoned with: 'After six matches I knew we wouldn't be relegated. After 12 matches I thought we could reach the play-offs and by the time we went to Derby County, I was confident we were in with a shout. The three games called off over Christmas didn't help and we had a bit of a rough ride, but those 27 points from nine wins on the trot put us back on top.'

Views of the management staff and players as to the key to the success differed widely, with Saxton citing the spirit in the camp as crucial: 'A lot of games stand out but after the 2–1 win at Oldham the team spirit in the dressing room was electric. There's only been a handful of games where we have had to have a go so I think that shows the excellent team effort it has been. We've now all got a challenge ahead. The Premiership is a challenge for the directors, the manager and the players.'

Many people still subscribe to the view that chairman Tom Cowie acted too hastily in sacking Alan Durban on 2 March 1984, even though a 2–1 defeat at Old Trafford left Sunderland without a win in seven games stretching back to New Year's Eve and only a four-point safety cushion from relegation. Relations with the chairman had been non-existent for some time and results over the last few weeks of the season would determine whether he would be offered a new contract. Said Alan Durban on the day of his dismissal:

> I was offered a one-year extension of my contract five weeks ago and the chairman says I have been too long in making a decision. At the end of the day I like to think I am fairly principled. The offer was made and I think the chairman was reasonably happy I did not accept it. I have not had a working relationship with him for months, so the decision to sack me has not come as a surprise. When I took the job, I knew that the chances of success in the First Division are

Player-of-the-season Richard Ord.

Welsh international Andy Melville enjoying a best-ever season.

Michael Gray, one of only two ever-presents in Sunderland's First Division Championship side.

Polish international Dariusz Kubicki, an ever-present at right back with a total of 118 appearances since moving from Aston Villa.

Dariusz Kubicki leads the way supported by (left to right) *Martin Scott, Kevin Ball and Lee Howey at Roker Park on 27 April 1996.*

Sunderland whizz-kid Michael Bridges proudly shows off his First Division Championship medal.

Sunderland manager Peter Reid shows his appreciation to coach Bobby Saxton for his part in winning the First Division Championship in the celebrations at Roker Park on 27 April 1996.

Peter Reid takes centre stage in the Sunderland dressing-room with (front, left to right) *Martin Scott, Dariusz Kubicki, Michael Gray.* Back row: *Kevin Ball, Alec Chamberlain, Craig Russell, Lee Howey, Richard Ord and Steve Agnew.*

Back row left to right: *Phil Gray, Martin Smith, Michael Bridges, Andy Melville, Alec Chamberlain, Lee Howey, Gareth Hall, Steve Agnew.* Front row: *Craig Russell, Dariusz Kubicki, Paul Bracewell, Kevin Ball, Richard Ord, Martin Scott, Michael Gray, Sam Aiston.*

Martin Scott in party mood along with Steve Agnew (centre) *and Michael Gray at Roker Park on 27 April 1996.*

An estimated 50,000 fans turned out to welcome the Sunderland players to a civic reception at the Seaburn Centre 24 hours after clinching the First Division Championship.

stacked against you – especially in view of the record here over the last 30 years. I looked at the situation at Sunderland and thought that apart from Alan Brown looking to the long-term, what success there had been had been done on a short-term basis. In the short-term, we brought in one or two players in Frank Worthington and Jimmy Nicholl, but we embarked on a long-term policy with little chance of immediate success. All I know is that when I arrived here the club had a lot of liabilities, but there are now players with assets who have won youth and Under-21 honours to justify the policy.

Pop Robson was immediately put in temporary charge for the home game with Arsenal the following afternoon, and a last-gasp penalty from Gary Rowell saved a point against the Gunners. Former long-serving full-back Len Ashurst, manager of Cardiff City, was officially appointed the new manager on Monday morning.

After a gap of 11 years, Durban is back at Roker relishing his new role and linking up again with Paul Bracewell and Pop Robson in the new-look management team. And he reckons they have a more than even chance of succeeding:

Every club has a chance every four or five years to take off but Sunderland didn't really take their chance last time after the 1992 FA Cup Final. But the opportunity is there and this backroom staff gives it a tremendous platform. Any club that defends well has a very good chance of staying up. The sides that have come straight back down like Swindon Town, Leicester City and Bolton Wanderers are the ones that have always conceded goals. But I have maintained all season when I see this team, and I only see it once a month because my scouting takes me elsewhere, it keeps improving, playing good football, and the atmosphere is second to none.

It's down to the manager. There's a good mix of experience and youth and every successful club needs three or four influential players to take it a long way. The best players influence those around them and, without mentioning names, Sunderland have them.

11

Tributes

Howard Kendall is not in the least surprised by Peter Reid reviving Sunderland's fortunes. And neither is he too surprised that Paul Bracewell has taken to his dual role like a duck to water.

Reid and Bracewell were the engine room of the successful Everton side of the 1980s managed by Kendall. Reid was an FA Cup winner and League Cup runner-up at Goodison Park in 1984; a First Division Championship winner, European Cup Winners' Cup winner and FA Cup runner-up a year later; First Division and FA Cup runner-up in 1986; with another First Division Championship win in 1987. Bracewell, too, won major honours at Everton, including England international honours in the World Cup in Mexico. Said Howard Kendall: 'They both played wing half and in that position you are in a good position to have a good look around you and see what is going on. I know Peter really well from our Everton days and I'm delighted he is doing so well. Peter is one of the game's winners. He always was as a player and now he has come through some adversity in management to emerge a winner in that job as well. There's no great secret to the way he has turned them round. They just needed a bit of organising, and Peter has done it superbly.'

Howard Kendall mounted a similar rescue operation at Bramall Lane where he took Sheffield United from the brink of relegation to mid-table respectability: 'We are a year behind Sunderland,' he said.

'What Peter Reid has done at Roker Park, I intend to do here. He saved them from relegation, which I have done here, and next year I want to be in the same position as Sunderland. I believe there are definite similarities between us and Sunderland. We've got the same ambition and potential.'

Though Howard Kendall warned of the size of the task ahead in the Premiership, he wants Sunderland fans to savour the achievements of winning promotion. He said:

> Enjoy it. Don't be moaning and talking about coming straight back down if there are not millions of pounds to spend. There is a gap between the Premiership and the rest, and Sunderland's objective will be survival. But if you are a big club with ambition, money is going to be made available for team strengthening. I think Sunderland should enjoy the moment rather than worry about how they will get on against Newcastle, Manchester United and the rest. I grew up in the north-east and know all about the passion that exists up there. And there's no doubt about it – it's going to be the place to be with three teams in the Premiership.

Terry Butcher, sacked by Coventry City after a disastrous spell as player-manager, fared no better at Roker Park even though he had given up the playing side to concentrate on his managerial duties only. Now a Radio Five and Sky Sports television pundit, when not pulling pints at his hotel in Scotland, Butcher hailed the achievements of Peter Reid:

> Sunderland has never looked back since I left. I suppose they did go backwards a bit and I would have loved a longer crack at it. In some ways, I envy Peter Reid, but it's better to have tried and failed than not to have tried at all. I respect him a lot as a manager. The only thing with him is his accent, I couldn't understand a word he was saying. We played together in the World Cup in Mexico. He is the type you want in the trenches with you. At the time, he only had a handful of caps, but there he was organising things and shouting instructions at people who had three times as many England appearances under their belts. But everybody respected him. He was a good player and his style of management reflects his playing style.

The endearing memory of Sunderland's 1973 FA Cup win is Bob Stokoe running across the Wembley turf to embrace goalkeeper Jimmy Montgomery. Stokoe has given up the jogging as he reaches pensionable age, but he hailed the transformation inspired by Peter Reid:

> I met Peter when he trained with Bury and the Sunderland job came out of the blue. He did a great job last season when most people suspected the club would go down. But it didn't happen and it will be great to see them back in the top flight. I can't wait to see the red and whites of Sunderland against the black and whites of Newcastle. There is talk that Sunderland will struggle in the Premiership if they don't spend a fortune. That may be the case but I don't think they will be bothering too much about that at the moment. Peter, his staff and the players should be allowed to enjoy what they have achieved. It is a wonderful time for them and they should savour it.

Bob Stokoe has always treasured that magical day his underdogs defeated Leeds – so much so he is reluctant to visit Wembley again. 'I want to take the memory with me. I don't want anything to spoil it. That's why I won't go back.'

Bob Stokoe was awarded the Freedom of Sunderland for his heroics of 1973, but not far behind in the popularity stakes of Roker fans is Charlie Hurley. Voted 'Player of the Century', the darling of the '60s urged the board to make Peter Reid the club's first Premiership signing:

> The Premiership is what the game is all about at the moment. For Sunderland to get there is a magnificent achievement but I think Peter Reid's side, even at this moment in time, will be in the middle band and hold their own.
>
> The first aim is solidarity in the Premiership because without a doubt it is a very difficult league. I would think the Premiership is three different leagues. The top eight at this moment in time will always win the Championship – the middle six or seven can hold their own and the bottom group will always struggle. But you can't go into the Premiership and just want to hold your own. What Sunderland need now is somebody to win the lottery after three roll-

overs and stick fifteen million pounds into the kitty. It's going to be very tough. Peter has done a fantastic job. To come here 15 months ago with the club in a relegation position and to finish winning the First Division Championship without spending much money has to be manager of the year stuff.

I have watched him talking to his players. He was like the Bomber [Alan Brown] who could create a lovely atmosphere. I love coming to Roker Park to reminisce about the goals I scored and the rickets I made. It's a lovely feeling and it's going to be very sad for a lot of football fans when they leave. Roker Park is a one-off. I played here in front of 63,000 fans quite regularly. But the game has gone into a completely different era. It is money driven. When we won promotion, teams had a chance of winning the championship the next season, like Leeds United did, but that won't happen now. Peter is a great pro though and when you consider what he has achieved in 15 months, what can he do in another four years?

King Charlie witnessed the presentation of the First Division Championship trophy to Kevin Ball and, bursting with pride, recalled the day in 1964 when he, too, celebrated promotion from the same division:

We have loved one another since 1957 and, while there were over 50,000 in the ground when we won promotion in 1964, the fervour is just the same. It's been a great day for me and a great day for the fans. When I played here the gates were over 50,000. I think it's a joke that only 22,000 were here – there must be room for another 10,000 on the terraces. The supporters are the ones who deserve the occasion, and they deserve a place back in the top flight.

I don't think Peter yet realises what he has got hold of here – it is a monster. If he gets it right, this club can be as big as anything in the Premiership, but it will cost a lot of money. What he needs immediately are Premiership-quality goalscorers. But, once he gets the right players in, the rewards will be tremendous.

Billy Hughes, another firm favourite with Sunderland supporters for his part in the 1973 FA Cup Final triumph, took a rare day off from his duties as steward of Stressholme Golf Club on the outskirts of

Darlington to savour the return to the big time: 'This is only the third Sunderland game I have seen this season,' he said. 'I have been very impressed with them and Peter Reid has got them very organised. He is the best thing that has happened to this club since sliced bread. It's not going to be easy, but they've got to stay in the Premiership next season – and fingers crossed they will.'

12

Celebrations

LONG before Kevin Ball stepped forward to receive the First Division Championship trophy from Endsleigh Football League president Gordon McKeag, the celebrations were in full swing. The fans were in high spirits and the fact Sunderland had to be satisfied with a second successive goalless home draw to mathematically deny Derby County the chance of the title was not going to stop the party. Ball, suspended for the game, wasn't prepared to miss out either. Decked out in his red-and-white shirt for the proudest day of his career, he brought up the rear with his manager.

Club stewards, dancing girls, ball boys and mascots formed a guard of honour for the players to make their grand entrance into the arena. First to acknowledge the raptures of a packed and frenzied Roker crowd were penalty king Martin Scott and ever-present Michael Gray. Dariusz Kubicki, the only other ever-present, and goalkeeper Alec Chamberlain were next up. Strikers Lee Howey and Craig Russell were followed by teenage pair Michael Bridges and Sam Aiston.

Central defender Andy Melville teamed up with Martin Smith, recalled to the substitutes bench after months on the sidelines recovering from a groin operation. Midfield pair Gareth Hall and Steve Agnew were next out, ahead of Player of the Year Richard Ord and assistant manager Paul Bracewell. David Kelly accepted a medal on behalf of Shay Given and John Mullin in the enforced absence of Paul Stewart.

The stage was then set for manager Peter Reid and his inspirational captain Kevin Ball to milk the applause of the crowd. And what a lovely touch from the manager when his players set off on their deserved lap of honour. An emotionally drained Reid made sure his 13-year-old daughter Louise would not miss out on the action either. A diehard Bolton Wanderers supporter, Louise was beckoned on to the middle of the pitch and she accompanied her proud dad around the pitch, too. 'The reaction of the supporters when we went round with the trophy was something I will certainly never ever forget,' said Reid. 'They were superb. It's been ten months' hard work and it's great to get a trophy to go up as champions. It's hard to put into words and it's something I find hard to believe. I think it's a tremendous achievement by everybody. Those scenes were brilliant. I haven't got words to describe the supporters. They are top class, the best.'

Sunderland's success proved too much for the dear old lady perched on top of the famous trophy. With the crowd going wild in the build-up to the official presentation, a gust of wind swept an advertising board off its feet. It hit the table and the trophy toppled over. Attempts to straighten the statue proved disastrous and, when Kevin Ball stepped forward to receive the trophy, the top piece was missing. According to League president Gordon McKeag, the famous old trophy has survived a few mishaps in the past. But Kevin Ball was adamant the accident was none of his doing: 'I want to quash here and now and deny any rumours that I went in for a 50/50 tackle on the dear old lady.'

Brothers Aubrey and George Parnaby are among the few Sunderland fans who remember the glory of the 1937 FA Cup-winning side. They watched Raich Carter lift the Cup in 1937 and Bobby Kerr in 1973 and have supported every one of the club's promotion campaigns. But they reckoned that the celebrations of 1996 compare with any of the great moments of the past. Aubrey, 75, of Hastings Hill, Sunderland, said: 'This is among the highlights of all things I have seen at Roker Park. We have seen a few championships, but this has been as good as any of them. I enjoyed seeing Charlie Hurley back at the club and watching Gary Rowell show how to convert penalties in the half-time interval. It was great to watch the players running around the pitch and Peter Reid having his moments of celebration. I think the fans appreciated the gesture of Kevin Ball, who took the trophy over to the disabled section to let the fans touch the trophy.'

George added: 'It wasn't a great game, but I was more pleased than anything else that we had won the Championship. Maybe the absence of Kevin Ball and Paul Stewart had its effect. It was a great day though – '37 and '73 were marvellous – but getting into the Premiership compares with those achievements.'

Councillor Fred Taylor, who helped set up the Boldon branch of the Sunderland Supporters' Association, said: 'When you think at the beginning of the season, setting up the Boldon branch was a bit of a struggle. Sunderland fans were so disillusioned after putting up with the last five seasons of underachievement; what has happened is just incredible. I'm glad we set the branch up this season; people who joined up when we were initially struggling have had a season to remember. After the match when the trophy was presented it was just brilliant, fantastic, and there were tears in my eyes. Congratulations to everyone involved with the club.'

A sea of red and white throbbed along the Sunderland coast to cheer Peter Reid and his players. An estimated 50,000 waited at the Seaburn Centre for a civic reception where they were congratulated by the Mayor of Sunderland, Eric Bramfitt. He said: 'A Premier League team in a Premier League city. Promotion would mean a "huge" boost for Wearsiders and "a wonderful impact" on the image of England's newest city across Europe.'

'Absolutely wonderful' was the verdict of Sunderland Council chief executive Colin Sinclair. 'It's really fantastic that the people of Sunderland turned out in such numbers to celebrate the championship.' Thousands more crowded around Roker Park to see the players board an open-top bus and hold the Cup aloft. Then they followed the coach to the Seaburn Centre. Singing and dancing, cheers and screams erupted the minute Peter Reid and his team boarded the bus and finally left after a series of encores on the Seaburn Centre balcony.

13

New Stadium

Sunderland will quit an antiquated Roker Park and move to the biggest new stadium ever to be built in England at the former Wearmouth Colliery pit site for the start of the 1997/98 season. The capacity of the all-seater stadium will eventually rise to 40,000 and enable the club to compete on financial terms at least with most of their Premiership rivals. The decision to move, first mooted in 1990, from one of the most famous grounds in the Football League was not taken lightly, but in the wake of the Taylor Report it was essential if the club were to survive.

The Taylor Report into the 1989 Hillsborough disaster, where 95 people died at the FA Cup semi-final between Liverpool and Nottingham Forest, changed the face of football for ever. Clubs with grounds which had seen little real change since the Second World War were told that, in the interests of safety, they had to become all-seater by August 1994, or else. Many froze at the cost of converting mass areas of terracing to seats and explored the viability of uprooting to a new stadium instead. Sunderland were among the first to declare their intentions to re-locate and ten sites were considered, nine in the green belt.

But immediately on unveiling plans for a multi-million-pound super stadium near the giant Nissan car plant, the development was beset with problems. The £45 million ground and adjoining leisure complex promised to create up to 2,000 jobs. The leisure package included a 12-screen cinema, 24-lane bowling alley, a nightclub, hotel, shopping centre, ice rink, tournament tennis court, boxing arena and 3,000 parking spaces in addition to the 8,000 set aside for the stadium.

Club officials promised fans a referendum would be held before any final decision was made to quit Roker Park. Director John Wood, who had been heavily involved in planning the move, explained the thinking behind the move and corrected some misconceptions. After all, the club was taking the heart and soul of Roker Park with them when they moved: the famous clock, lattice work from the stand and even the turf itself would be transported to the new site: 'There are a lot of peoples' lives wrapped up in Roker Park and a lot of ashes on that pitch. It is only right they should find a place in our new home. We have spent a long time preparing this. It has been two years since its inception and I'm very confident we will see it through. There are a lot of private investors interested in putting money into that.'

John Wood cut through some of the rumours and misconceptions in a frank assessment of the project, stressing that:

- The stadium and leisure complex plans, unmatched anywhere in the country, would not cost the club or the taxpayer a penny.
- There is absolutely no gain for anybody associated with Sunderland AFC.
- The board's aim is to assemble a team good enough to play at the new ground.
- The local workforce benefits with 2,000 permanent new jobs.
- The club will answer any valid objections. 'We have covered all the points and this is the only way forward,' confirmed John Wood.

The club allowed 12 months notice for planning approval and looked to begin work on the massive complex in April 1994, to be completed for use in time for the 1995/96 season.

Said John Wood: 'We simply could not redevelop Roker Park into a 40,000 all-seater stadium. That's why we hit on this mix. The revenue will come from the retail sector plus the arena and grant aid – the bulk of that from Brussels. There is a unique link between the stadium and the arena. There will be nothing like this anywhere in the country – not even at Wembley. We sat down and thought, why not have the best sports complex in the world? Now we are determined to follow it through.'

The city council paved the way for the move with the decision to release a major green belt site, but a rebel Roker Supporters Trust group insisted Roker Park should be redeveloped at a cost of £25 million, sinking the pitch 15 feet and doubling the size of the stands to increase capacity to 40,000. Nissan voiced fears of traffic congestion with engineering director Les Nicholls claiming: 'Maintaining good road transport access to the plant is essential for our business. Selection of Sunderland as a centre for car manufacturing was influenced by many factors – not least of which was the excellent infrastructure. Nissan are now in detailed discussions with Sunderland Football Club and its traffic experts to assess the impact of the project, which has parking provision for almost 20,000 cars. The company believes it is essential that a traffic assessment is made before a submission for outline planning is made.' Sunderland chairman Bob Murray retorted: 'Nissan will have problems with or without the stadium. The roads in the area, such as the A19, are going to need improving anyway due to their increased output. There is no way we wish to hold Nissan back at all. The region needs this facility. It needs a European centre of entertainment and leisure excellence. It will kick-start the decade and bring new jobs and investment into the region.'

But Nissan officially objected to the scheme following an independent traffic survey commissioned on their behalf and carried out by consultants W.S. Atkins, which claimed a 30,000 crowd at the planned stadium would paralyse local roads. Nissan's director of engineering, Les Nicholls, said the club had been unable to allay fears about traffic snarl-ups which could cripple the production at the award-winning car plant. He said the survey confirmed the company's fears that the road network would not cope with the extra burden from the complex, with or without its planned leisure and retail developments. But Bob Murray replied: 'How can they object before even seeing the plans? All the advisers, all the people in the region are more confident than ever that this mega, brave development for the people of the north-east will take place. It's going to happen. The club is surprised that a company with the international standing of Nissan has not taken steps to secure its long-term future in the region if expansion was a realistic option.'

Newcastle United chairman and mastermind of the MetroCentre, Sir John Hall, joined the growing list of doubters and objecters, blasting the scheme as just a glorified soccer club planned for the wrong place. He said a new Roker Park would offer nothing for the region. Sir John hit out over the possibility of European grants coming to Wearside, and not Tyneside, to help pay for the £120 million project.

> I have looked at the plans, and we at Newcastle are doing exactly the same already. We will have ample conference facilities for the whole region when we are finished redeveloping St James's Park. There are already three retail parks in the area, and the MetroCentre, and we do not need any more. It is a misuse of green belt to develop retail parks on it. The economy will not sustain it, and I find it difficult to accept investors will come up with the cash.
>
> Years ago I pushed for a regional stadium for Sunderland and Newcastle and it was scoffed at. Now we have a duplication of what is on offer by two clubs. The site proposed is in the wrong place. It has no rail or Metro links. Newcastle has direct rail and Metro links, air links, better hotel accommodation and is already offering facilities nearly every day of the week. We will be saying such when we put in our own, stronger bid for Euro-cash. If any site was to be redeveloped by Sunderland, there is a much better one between Washington and Gateshead – one hundred acres in size with close Metro links already existing. Having looked at the plans there is nothing unique about the scheme. It is just a glorified soccer stadium.

Bob Murray dismissed the bitter criticism levied against the club by Sir John.

> The complex is recognised as being of regional and national importance. It means new investment, permanent jobs and will give the region a multi-purpose exhibition, conference and entertainment centre of international status. The complex will be home to a

European stadium and a 12,000-seater arena – both with full, superb support.

Anybody with the full interests of the north-east at heart should carefully consider their own position before questioning a complex with so many benefits to the region. Three years have now been spent on bringing the development to this stage. We are fully aware that the football elements of the project receive no European assistance – this we have known from the outset.

By September 1993, the club was forced to scrap plans for the shopping complex in a bid to squash opposition to its super stadium. Bob Murray explained the shopping element of his ambitious scheme had been axed because of his determination to protect Sunderland city centre and business trading there. He revealed the club had clinched major franchise and sponsorship deals which would offset the cash lost by scrapping the shopping plans. He also revealed that the motel, the only part of the scheme to be built in South Tyneside, had also been axed after the council expressed concern.

Nissan emerged as the only major stumbling block and director John Wood took up the challenge by launching a scathing attack on the club's would-be neighbours: 'Nissan's attitude has been inflexible. It's a great shame that the future of the region is in the hands of other people thousands of miles away in Tokyo. We have offered them every opportunity with regard to land around that site.' Nissan managing director Ian Gibson hit back in an open letter: 'We have never opposed the concept of the proposed Regional and European Centre and, indeed, would like to see such a centre on Wearside. Since discussions began with Bob Murray in August 1992, Nissan has always tried to find a way to accept your plans for this major development, which shares a boundary with our own industrial site. We remain as an objector to the current proposals because of their adverse effect on our business, but will, of course, abide by the final decision of any public inquiry.'

By January 1994, the Department of Transport (DOT) expressed traffic fears and ordered the club back to the drawing board. City councillors were told of:

•The need for 'major improvements' at Testo's roundabout to cope with predicted traffic flows.

•The 'inadequacy' of proposed access arrangements, and the 'implications for queueing and congestion on the A19'.
•The 'close proximity of access and junctions along the A19 and the implicationsfor signing and safety'.

The DoT said it could not accept the proposed highway arrangements which effectively reduced, in some cases, weaving (lane-changing) lengths between junctions on the A19 to as little as 30 per cent of the recommended distances.

The Department stressed that: 'Road safety is the one aspect of our work which we cannot compromise.' It warned that unless the stadium traffic could be accommodated safely, it would be forced to order the city council to refuse the planning application.

The following month the DoT gave the thumbs up to the stadium, but with crowds initially reduced to just 20,000, less than half of the planned 48,000 capacity. And they would not be filled unless the DoT pumped government cash into a massive fly-over at Testo's roundabout. The two key conditions imposed by the DoT:

•Before work starts on the complex, the club's access must be completed – including roads over the A19 and peak-period traffic lights at Testo's roundabout.
•Maximum crowds are to be restricted to 20,000 until the DoT decides to go ahead with the massive, split-level Testo's junction. Only days before the city planning bosses were due to meet (10 March) Nissan chiefs made a final 'think-again' plea. Nissan claimed the stadium plan had three major drawbacks:
•It kills off any prospect of future single-site expansion for the firm in the event of a worldwide upturn in the car industry, which is forecast in eastern and southern Europe over the next decade. Nissan says that is because its existing 800-acre site is developed almost to saturation point, and it is hemmed in on all its other boundaries.
•It will create traffic chaos on the roads leading in and out of the site, since both the stadium and Nissan will effectively become a single destination point for visitors and workers alike.
•Nissan claims that the future prosperity of both itself and the stadium complex will be hit by the traffic complications

involved. Company bosses say if major arena events, crucial crowd-pulling football fixtures and factory shift changes coincide, the result will be even worse traffic congestion.

Mr Gibson said Nissan's objections were being made reluctantly, but said the company had no choice but to fight for its own future and that of its workers. He added: 'We urge the decision-makers to weigh fully and carefully the effect such a development would have on Nissan's business and its contribution to the future prosperity of the city.'

On 10 March 1994 Sunderland City Council recommended to approve the stadium plans, but it was only half-time in the long-running saga with Nissan who, bitterly disappointed, determined to battle on. Nissan's Les Nicholls said: 'I think my disappointment stems from the fact that each of our concerns, such as traffic problems, has been accepted, documented and verified, but there appears to be no solution to it. We will abide by the final decision reached through the proper procedures, but frankly, as an engineering director having to make the factory live with that, I'm dismayed.' He said Nissan would never have moved to the area if it had known what lay in store. Club chiefs pledged that if the scheme goes ahead, they will work alongside Nissan to ensure their stadium traffic does not affect the company's transport operations.

A week later Environment Secretary John Gummer set the ball rolling on whether to order a public inquiry. The plan has to be approved by Mr Gummer since it marks a major departure from the city council's ten-year development strategy for the city, and it is earmarked for a green belt site. On 25 March, Mr Gummer duly 'called in' the controversial application. Both sides welcomed the decision. Sunderland director John Wood: 'This is the timeframe we were always working in – it's not the unforeseen. What's happening is exactly what we thought would happen.' Nissan spokesman John Neilson said: 'We welcome the fact that the proposal has been called in by the Secretary of State. We believe that a possible public inquiry will spark a wider review of alternative solutions, other than building the stadium on Nissan's doorstep. It is thought Sunderland Football Club's scheme will create 250 jobs, and while we would never knock that, we feel that the 10,000 jobs related to Nissan must be given priority.'

On 25 August 1994, club officials asked the Department of the Environment to put the public inquiry into the disputed A19 site on hold while they looked into the possibility of the 40-acre site at Wearmouth Colliery as an alternative. Director John Wood said: 'There is little doubt the A19 is the best site. We have always said we will investigate all suitable alternatives and we feel it is prudent to look into the possibility of relocating to Wearmouth. We are being open-minded, seeing what else is available. I am sure the inspector at the public inquiry will ask us if we have looked at other sites.'

The months dragged on and it was not until 9 February 1995 that Sunderland Football Club decided to abandon the A19 project in favour of a move to Wearmouth, but again fears were expressed over traffic congestion. The transport implications of a 34,000 all-seater development so close to the city centre will mean modification of existing roads as well as some new construction, including the building of three new roundabouts.

Residents will be encouraged to use the Metro system and two new stations at Roker and Monkwearmouth will be built in 1998 within 500 metres and 450 metres of the new stadium. To encourage use of the Metro, the club is exploring the possibility of introducing combined match and Metro tickets for an initial period.

A restricted parking scheme could be introduced to stop supporters parking in residential streets near the stadium two hours before a match. Residents would be issued with permits that would allow them to park outside their homes. The Council Millennium bid also proposes a new footbridge across the River Wear to allow access to the stadium from the south of the city.

The new scheme was still in the early stages when Bob Murray ruled the club out of any link with plans for a £70 million leisure complex and stadium at Ryhope. Developers say the stadium would have the potential to be the biggest in the country.

But Murray reaffirmed his commitment to build a stadium for the club on the Wearmouth pit site:

> There's no way we can be side-tracked at this crucial eleventh hour and I am confident that no one would expect a city unitary plan to be turned upside down at the drop of a hat. I do not believe these latest proposals, which I have not seen apart from learning a few

rather sketchy details from a press statement, will do anything for our development apart from attempting to spoil our commitment. The council votes on 13 July and the development corporation on 24 July, and the future of our scheme is in their capable hands. I am confident they will make the right decision for the people of Sunderland, giving us a mandate to pursue our ambition to give the city a stadium it deserves and will be proud of.

Plans for the site next to dual carriageway A1018 joining Ryhope with the A19 were submitted to the city council on 3 July 1995, and developers say the scheme should create 500 full- and part-time jobs. The ambitious scheme included:

- A £30 million stadium, initially with a 40,000 capacity capable of extending to 56,000, with a maximum-size pitch, 40 executive boxes, banqueting facilities and a soccer hall of fame.
- An 80-bedroom three-star hotel.
- A multi-screen cinema with up to 14 screens.
- Fast food restaurants, to be occupied by giant chains like McDonald's and Burger King, along with bar facilities.
- A large health and fitness club, including sauna, spa, swimming, and gymnasium facilities.
- An enormous car park with spaces for 6,500 cars and 80 coaches, with a possible second ten-acre car park across the A1018 for away fans.

Project director Colin Lynas, of Stockton-based Crouch Hogg Waterman civil engineering firm, said the new stadium and leisure complex could be largely built within a year once permission is gained. And the businessmen behind the Matthew Fox Partnership say they already have secured big bank cash backing for the 74-acre complex.

A fans' action group urged the club to consider the scheme. Supporters Action For Change spokesman Steve Marley said: 'Given the club's failure over the past two years to build a new stadium and the objections already registered against the Wearmouth site, surely a third-party proposal is worth at least a second glance and an assessment based on its merits.' To convince fans the Wearmouth scheme was the best available, however, the club arranged trips for local residents to Middlesbrough's new Riverside Stadium, designed along similar lines. Two trips took Southwick residents and supporters to Teesside to give them an idea what the Wearmouth Stadium would look like. Gary Stevens, chairman of Sunderland Football Club's liaison group, said: 'Middlesbrough's stadium is quite impressive, from what I can see. And because the same design team has worked on Sunderland's stadium, I am sure the development will be just as impressive.' John Cowley, of J.M. Cowley Insurance Services, who was also on the trip as a member of the North-East Chamber of Trade, said: 'There's no doubt in my mind that we have to move from Roker Park. It's unrealistic to think anything can be done to Roker Park.' Lesley Coates, the club's corporate communications manager, who organised the trip, said: 'The club was eager for people to see Middlesbrough's stadium at first hand so they could appreciate how impressive a new stadium would be in Sunderland.'

On 13 July 1995, city planners threw their weight behind the Wearmouth scheme when they officially gave the go-ahead but attached conditions over roads and traffic. Bob Murray vowed: 'The issue of roads is one which we will not let defeat us. The Wearmouth plan has been hailed as a magnet for regeneration, and we must now grasp the nettle and sort out the highways issue.' Despite a warning from council leader Bryn Sidaway that the authority could not fund the improvements, Mr Murray added: 'The council has indicated that they will be helpful in finding the money, which is paramount to the success of the project.'

The next hurdle to be overcome also won the backing of development chiefs. The Tyne and Wear Development Corporation (TWDC) indicated it was in favour of approving the 34,000-seat stadium. The application must now be forwarded to the Secretary of State for the Environment, John Gummer, who will decide whether the corporation itself can grant overall approval. A TWDC spokesman said: The corporation expects to hear the Minister's response by the end of August and, on the assumption that it has not been called in for a public inquiry, the board will consider the application at the earliest opportunity.'

Bob Murray described the TWDC vote as 'Yet another major step in the right direction. We have always said that a project as important to Sunderland as the stadium must be a partnership between the club, the council, corporation and people.'

The scheme was back under the microscope again when a heated meeting of the full council voted 36 to 27 in favour. It was the third vote on the stadium proposals, and the second time Sunderland City Council had debated the plans. But city councillors north of the city were adamant the full council should reject the plan. Cllr Bryan Charlton said: 'Who in their right mind would think about building a football stadium so near a city centre?'

Sunderland MP Bill Etherington urged Environment Secretary John Gummer to order a public inquiry, expressing his opposition to the scheme: 'A football stadium could hardly be classed as the kind of inner-city regeneration that John Gummer is talking about. The streets are already very bad with traffic every Saturday, and as bad as it is now, I think it would be even worse if this goes ahead. The present ground is very badly positioned for traffic, but I don't think Wearmouth is any better.'

John Gummer, however, decided not to order a public inquiry, which could have delayed the project for many months, and the rival plan at Ryhope was scuppered. Speaking during a short holiday in Jersey, Bob Murray said: 'It's brilliant. I am delighted with the news and the fact the D of E has made such a quick decision. We have come a long way and there are still hurdles to overcome, but we can see the finishing line now.'

A TWDC spokeswoman said planning approval now rested on the club signing a 'one hundred and six agreement' – a legal deal imposing four major conditions on the club. The club must:

- •Demolish Roker Park and clear the site for redevelopment once the new stadium is available.
- •Produce a formal scheme on how they will run the 2,500 space stadium car park.
- •Use 'all reasonable endeavours' to negotiate with public transport operators and put in place an efficient network to get fans to and from home matches.
- •Use 'all reasonable endeavours' to work with the highways authority and assess the impact of parking and to ease the problems, using measures that 'must be considered cost-effective, feasible and legally enforceable'.

On 31 October, 1995, Bob Murray announced the cost of building the Wearmouth Stadium had risen by two million pounds to £14 million because of improved furnishings and fittings. The funding of the stadium breaks down like this:

- Bob Murray will underwrite £3 million.
- Borrowing facilities of £3 million in the form of a Term Loan secured on the freehold stadium, owned by the club.
- A Football Grant Trust in line with that of Millwall and Middlesbrough (estimated at £3 million).
- Commercial and marketing funds achieved from naming rights, global marketing and sponsorship of £3.5 million.
- Net proceeds from the sale of Roker Park, £500,000.

The £3.25 million grant from the Football trust is the biggest paid out to any football club in the country. The Trust offered a £2.5 million grant, £250,000 from its FA Contribution Account and an interest-free loan of £500,000. Peter Lee, chief executive of the Football Trust, said: 'One of the Taylor Report's major recommendations was for clubs to consider relocation as a way of solving the major problems associated with cramped sites and limited amenities. Relocation is a huge undertaking and Sunderland can count on the Trust for maximum support. We commend the club's far-sighted proposals and determined approach to provide the highest standard of safety for their supporters.'

The final planning hurdle was removed on 13 November 1995, with Bob Murray hailing the go-ahead as 'a historic milestone for Sunderland Football Club'.

He continued: 'Roker Park has served us well over the years. But we all recognise that to compete at the highest levels in the future, we need a stadium that will allow us to generate the levels of income that are required in the modern game. We need to compete with other big city clubs and the decision by the Tyne and Wear Development Corporation is a major step forward in this direction.'

Four construction companies were invited to tender for the stadium after interviews by club directors and the project managers, Drivers Jonas:

- Ballast Needham Construction Ltd – a nationwide company with worldwide links, whose contract experience includes the £80 million, 50,000-seater Amsterdam Arena.
- Birse, whose stadium expertise includes Blackburn Rovers' Ewood Park, the Kippax Stand at Manchester City and the £18 million three-tier North Stand at Manchester United's Old Trafford ground.
- Taylor Woodrow plc – recent work includes redevelopment of Ibrox and Nottingham Forest and the construction of the 30,000-seater Riverside Stadium for Middlesbrough.
- Tilbury Douglas construction, whose projects include Murrayfield Stadium in Edinburgh and the Sheffield International Arena.

No sooner had the dust settled than Bob Murray dropped another bombshell by announcing he wanted to increase the capacity of the stadium to 40,000, adding that he will only put in the extra seats in 1999, when the city's Metro link is up and running. He said he wanted to avoid the problems experienced by Newcastle and Middlesbrough, where loyal fans have been denied seats and season tickets because the stadiums have not been big enough to cope with demand.

The capacity of the stadium is restricted by the TWDC to 29,000 until the club sorts out its parking. Project manager Graham Fryer said that by building the bigger structure immediate savings could be gained, and added: 'There are a lot of benefits in planning terms to incorporate the greater capacity at this stage.' The appearance of the stadium would not be altered – except for an increase of 15 metres in width. Bob Murray said:

> I wouldn't wish to see any loyal Sunderland supporters become a casualty of success, either in terms of access to the club or affordability. We do not wish to see Wearside locked out of the new stadium; we must learn from the experiences of other clubs and not copy their mistakes.
>
> We think Newcastle have built a stadium for today and not tomorrow. They have obviously got their sums wrong and we are trying to get them as right as possible. Middlesbrough have not had one League game below capacity at their new Riverside Stadium and I believe they have got plans to extend already. Sunderland,

Newcastle and Middlesbrough used to go up and down like yo-yos because they did not have the resources, but this won't happen again. What we are saying is we will be putting down the fifth biggest stadium in England on an old pit site. We want to compete and we are not shy to admit that Newcastle and Middlesbrough influenced our decision.

In other places they build on city parks and in green belt areas. Here we are having trouble bringing a £14 million development in a none-too-healthy area of a city with no city investment going into it. It's on a plate and that can't be bad for a city and the people the councillors represent. We have also promised affordable football at the new stadium and this has always been based on no reduction in capacity. Obviously if the capacity is 29,000 we can't offer the envisaged pricing structure – it will affect the fans' pockets. We can't compromise at any stage – this is a stadium of European significance. We have taken a once-in-a-hundred-years decision and we have to think like a big city club and build a stadium that is fit for the 21st century.

We have got to balance affordability with the corporate line. The £14 million is in place, but it is not in the bank. We don't want to get caught in the middle, but the major factor is going to be football. There will be no pop concerts at the new stadium – that is for arenas – what we are building is a football stadium. We don't want an elitist club but people have to realise our total income last year was a record £5½ million. Our turnover can increase six fold to over £30 million – that's how big the new stadium can be.

The only decision that had to be made, has been made. Roker Park is flat out. If we sold out every match day, our turnover from 7,000 seats and 16,000 standing would only generate £7 million. We could not spend £5 million on one player and generate the cash. Roker Park has served us well, but it's gone. We've got 14 private boxes in poor condition whereas the new stadium will have 50 executive boxes including fax machines, telephones and private bar facilities.

Sunderland's financial plight was underlined when the accounts for the financial year ending 31 May 1995 revealed a loss of nearly £85,000 and a soaring bank overdraft in excess of £2 million.

With plans for the stadium gathering momentum, a consortium of foreign-based businessmen tested Murray's earlier resolve to place his majority holding on the market. Four of the seven consortia, tired of waiting for the outcome of protracted negotiations with Portsmouth chairman Martin Gregory, switched their attentions to Premiership-bound and new stadium-bound Sunderland. But Sunderland's chief executive, John Fickling, informed them the club was no longer for sale:

> I have spoken to the guy. He asked me if Sunderland Football Club was still for sale and I said I think you are six to twelve months out of date. And that's it. It never went any further than that. He asked me a straight question and I gave him a straight answer. I think they were all geared up for Portsmouth and, having been let down, were looking for somebody else.
>
> The funders of the new stadium need the comfort that certain people are going to be around. The last thing they want is instability. Nobody is going to lend you money if this one or that is going to disappear. As Bob rightly said, once the new ground has happened, the whole football club is on a different level. There is the position the whole thing will be reviewed – it's not to say it will be – but the revenue stream of the club is going to be different.
>
> There has been a lot of uncertainty. Twelve months ago people thought this club was dead and buried. But there is renewed spirit. What is coming from the boardroom is echoing this and that has not happened in the past. There is an attitude and a will to succeed.'

Bob Murray was confident control of the club would remain in the hands of the current board for the next two years:

> We can't stop rumours. The club is on a roll and we know we are going to be seen as more than just stadium developers. We have got to get the stadium up and provide Peter Reid with the ammunition that he needs eventually. My pledge is there and it's there beyond the completion of the stadium. Nobody is coming in now. The team (the current directors) is going to stay until the stadium is up and open. I can't see boardroom changes before then unless somebody comes in with BIG money for the playing side

and adds to the pot. I am going nowhere. We have got to make the stadium reality and stay in the Premiership.

Fears were expressed that the former pit site would not be suitable for a 40,000 seat football stadium. Preliminary findings of a top-level report shows the site itself has 'little soil contamination' and is not above mine workings.

The tenders were opened in the presence of members of the Football Trust and on 27 March 1996 it was announced leading Dutch construction group Ballast Wiltshire had been awarded the contract. Said Bob Murray: 'Ballast Wiltshire has a proven track record in stadia construction. We will draw upon their skills, expertise and experience to ensure not only is Sunderland the biggest new stadium, but also the best.'

A few days later the club received a double boost when Environment Secretary John Gummer gave the thumbs up the increased capacity stadium and officials agreed a lucrative two-year kit contract worth more than £1 million with existing sponsors Avec. The club's marketing and commercial development manager Grahame McDonnell said: 'The deal we have agreed is the biggest in the Endsleigh League and will rank high against teams in the Premiership.'

On 25 April, the club announced the cost of building the stadium had risen to £15 million due to minor changes to the architectural structure and gave Ballast Wiltshire the green light to begin work. The signing of the official agreement took place on site. Bob Murray declared:

> There's no turning back. We are committed to moving. There have been many historic sporting moments at Sunderland over the years; however, only once in a hundred years do we ever consider moving home. We are delighted to be working with Ballast Wiltshire, they share our goals and are committed to our vision. They have the pedigree and skills to make Sunderland's new stadium the best in the country, bar none.
>
> We, as a club, must get this cathedral right. It is so prominent and it is going to stand over the city for the next one hundred years and will be everybody's pride and joy. It is a culmination of four years'

hard work. It is very rewarding and I know everybody is going to feel part of it.

It will be a catalyst for other developments both inside and outside of Sunderland because its publicity appeal will be on a European scale. The stadium makes a statement about which direction Sunderland as a city is heading.

Chief executive John Fickling was just as excited at the prospect of moving to a new ground in a prime position of the city: 'Clubs building new stadiums generally have to move to the edge of town. But, as a result of this land becoming available, we are in the unique position of coming closer to the heart of Sunderland. The colliery was important to the economy and it is sad that it had to close. But football is also a major part of the area's lifeblood, so it is appropriate that we should be switching to the site.'

14

Medals

The Football League criteria is for 19 medals to be cast for the champions of any division, and Sunderland had no hesitation in requesting an additional four to be cast to ensure no player who qualifies would miss out.

Qualification is 25 per cent of games (i.e. 12 appearances) and though only 18 players are entitled to receive a medal, they were four short. The manager, physio and secretary are entitled to a medal and two are to be awarded at the club's discretion. But for injury, David Kelly would have qualified while John Mullin, a regular substitute in the early stages of the season, would also have been in the frame if not injured.

The 18 players who qualified for a medal were: Steve Agnew, Sam Aiston, Kevin Ball, Paul Bracewell, Michael Bridges, Alec Chamberlain, Shay Given, Phil Gray, Michael Gray, Gareth Hall, Lee Howey, Dariusz Kubicki, Andy Melville, Richard Ord, Craig Russell, Martin Scott, Martin Smith and Paul Stewart.

The medal helped ease the pain for Phil Gray for missing out on the last 13 games of the season. Transfer-listed at his own request, the £775,000 signing from Luton Town three years ago ended the season out of contract, determined to keep his options open.

> Hopefully, I have not played my last game for the club. I have no
> regrets coming here and have really enjoyed myself. Obviously I am

disappointed to have missed out on playing my part in promotion, but I am delighted for the rest of the lads and the supporters.

I am gutted, but a championship medal is a nice consolation to go with the 17 caps I have won for Northern Ireland. I have no idea what is going to happen. The manager will want to bring new players in, and while I haven't signed a contract, I have been offered one.

This has been the happiest time of my career and I don't regret signing for one minute. All I want now is to be fit for next season. I was playing as well as any time since I came here before the groin operation and I am in no hurry to leave. The new contract I have been offered is not just about money, but also the length of it.

Martin Scott, signed from Bristol City in an exchange deal valued at £750,000 the previous season, breezes into the Premiership chasing a hat-trick of medals:

I won a Fourth Division Championship medal at Rotherham in the 1989 season and I thought it was great. Bobby Saxton has been in the game for 30 years and has three championship medals – one for every ten years. I have two and hopefully a hat-trick is not too far away. You've got to have ambitions and right now that's to stay in the Premiership as long as possible and win something while we're there. The Premiership holds no fears and I am not scared. I've milked what's happened this season and my parents were so proud and delighted when they attended the celebrations. I knew when I came to Sunderland I was joining a big club and looked forward to days like this. For it to happen in the first 16 months of coming here is brilliant. It's happened at a perfect time for me but I don't think the younger lads realise what a great thing it is for them. It's a dream come true for me.Ever since I was young I have wanted to play in the top division and I must admit it's taken me longer than I expected. But I am relishing the prospect and that's what I have aimed for all my career. I came into a struggling team but this season from day one we have been the best team in the division. We play the best football and what else has helped is we have closed teams down and have worked as a team. It's been good teamwork, we've kept clean sheets and we've rolled our sleeves up and got stuck in when we've had to.

We are all in it together, not just the eleven players who go out there, but all the staff. We've all had a job to do and we've gone out and done it. I've been asked what was the key to our success and for me it was winning those nine games on the trot. Our points total just rocketed and we got ourselves into a tremendous position at the right time.'

Steve Agnew would willingly have settled for another crack at the play-offs after a personal nightmare start to the season. Crocked at the end of the previous campaign shortly after Peter Reid arrived to start the Roker revolution, the experienced midfielder firmly believed the summer break would cure an Achilles problem. But the injury flared up again in the first week of the new campaign with an operation the only course of action. It was a long haul back for a player who has been involved with both Blackburn Rovers and Leicester City reaching the Premiership after missing automatic promotion:

It's a great achievement by everybody at the club coming off the back of what happened last season. At the start of the season we felt we were capable of finishing in the top six and qualifying for the play-offs. I think most of our supporters would have settled for that but I am absolutely delighted for them that we finished in top spot. It's just a dream really.

For me the turning point was the game at Portsmouth. I scored first and I honestly thought we were going to win. But they scored twice and it looked as though we were going to lose when Lee Howey popped up with an injury-time equaliser. The away games at Southend, Oldham and Birmingham were all solid wins and it's performances like that which win you championships. We did not play as well in the last few home games as we know we can, but, rather than lose, we hung in there to get a result each time. If we had not been so tight defensively, which is reflected in the number of goals we conceded, we would not have won the title. It was a big weight off everybody not to be in the play-offs because they are big pressure games, just like a Cup final, and they become so nerve-racking. We did it the proper way and proved over 46 games that we were the best side in the division.

All I want to do now is savour what we have achieved. I only had a few months in the Premiership with Leicester City before I was transferred to Sunderland. They are all big games in the Premiership and I would imagine that Roker Park will be a sell-out next season.

I missed out on a Wembley medal in the play-offs through injury and it's a great feeling to get my hands on one at last. It's something I will always treasure.

Kevin Ball suffered the heartache of relegation in his first season at Sunderland after a £350,000 move from Portsmouth. But six years on he just can't wait for another bash at life in the top flight: 'I have always wanted another crack at the Premier League. I am going to enjoy the close season then gear myself up for next season. I've always wanted more than anything else for our supporters to finish top dogs, and that's what we've done. We had an open-top bus ride after the 1992 Cup Final, but we had nothing to show for it even though the turn-out was frightening. Something like this has been long overdue for our supporters and I'm delighted for them, the manager and the players.'

Ball was only one of two players brought in – striker Peter Davenport from Middlesbrough was the other – when Sunderland won promotion in 1990, and the lack of investment cost the club dearly.

But Kevin is confident the club is geared to take off this time and make up for the personal disappointment last time round:

> Whoever is in control of this club from top to bottom it's got to be fantastic for them because they can plot the course and it's got to be done right. But things are really looking up at Sunderland.
>
> At the end of last season it was 'here we go again' and we just got ourselves out of trouble. Promotion has been a fantastic achievement and next season it's important everything is planned the right way. I come from the south coast and the fans are not the same down there. Football is not as high-profile and people tend to look at the game as a leisure activity. In the north-east, football is a way of life and more people want to be associated with the club. I know it's an old cliché, but I would love to end my career here – not that I am thinking of hanging up my boots yet. I've learnt never to set targets and I just want to keep playing as long as I can.

Richard Ord scooped more player-of-the-year awards than any of his colleagues to finally prove himself a centre-back of genuine class after several seasons of mediocrity in several different positions. The former England Under-21 international had lost his way until the arrival of Peter Reid, who restored his confidence, switched him to his favourite role and made him captain in the absence of Kevin Ball. Ord recalled:

> I played 40-odd games when I was 18 and I think it went to my head a bit. I should have buckled down a bit more. I've had a couple of wayward years but that's behind me now. I think it is always going to be hard for players if the club hasn't paid a fee for them and for a while I just ended up getting a bit down-hearted. The championship means a lot to everyone at the club but I think it has to mean more to the local players because they have grown up with the fans – I've supported them since I was a kid. I think it went against me in the early stages of my career. I used to worry that everybody was watching me because I knew a lot of people on the terraces, and when you think like that, your performances can suffer. But I've matured a lot and my wife Sonia and one-year-old son Liam have helped me to do that. They have really helped me settle down.

But while settling down into a family routine has helped his game, Dickie Ord has no hesitation in paying tribute to Peter Reid for its transformation: 'I think everything he touches turns to gold. Every decision he has made seems to come right for him. I would not have been where I am today if it wasn't for him and he said straight away he'd stick by me in the side which really boosted my confidence. He said he couldn't believe I was playing left-back and he told me he thought I could become one of the best centre-halves in the country. This time round, though, I'm not letting it go to my head. I'm a lot more relaxed than I was and the family have made me realise that football isn't the only thing in life.'

Dariusz Kubicki turned his back on tempting offers from America and his native Poland in favour of playing in the Premier League again: 'I have had offers to play in the newly formed American League. But I am not interested, I am happy here. If I was struggling it would be a different matter. I want to stay in England at the moment. My family are happy here and ideally I want to play in the Premiership with Sunderland. There has been interest from Poland, but without being big-headed, I know there will always be a job back home. I am a respected name over there as I have played so many games for my country. If, and when, I do go back, I know I will be able to get a job.'

Appearances 1995/96

	Lge	LCup	FA Cup	Sub	Goals
Agnew	26	1	1	4	6
Aiston	4	0	0	11	0
Angell	2	1	0	0	1
Armstrong	0	0	0	2	0
Atkinson	5	3	0	2	0
Ball	35	4	1	1	4
Bracewell	38	4	2	0	0
Bridges	2	0	0	13	4
Chamberlain	29	4	2	0	0
Cooke	6	0	0	0	0
Given	17	0	0	0	0
Gray (Martin)	4	1	0	5	0
Gray (Michael)	46	4	2	0	4
Gray (Phil)	28	4	2	4	9
Hall	8	0	0	6	0
Howey	17	1	0	12	5
Kelly	9	1	1	1	2
Kubicki	46	4	2	0	0
Melville	40	2	2	1	4
Mullin	5	1	0	6	1
Ord	41	3	2	1	1
Russell	35	1	2	9	14
Scott	43	3	2	0	6
Smith	9	2	1	14	2
Stewart	11	0	0	1	1
Luton (og)	1				
Preston (og)		1			

15

The Media Reaction

Media attention in the north-east is considered to be more intense than any other area of the country with the managers of the three big clubs expected to be available for interviews on a daily basis. Some handle press conferences better than others but Peter Reid has a foot in the door when it comes to acknowledging the role of sports journalists: his brother-in-law Peter Mensforth is sports editor of the *Bolton Evening News*!

Covering a professional football team has its perks but, contrary to popular belief, it's certainly not the bed of roses many are led to believe with a journalist's social life constantly disrupted throughout the course of a season. True, admittance to matches is free, a seat in the stands is guaranteed and most clubs are generous with refreshments during the interval and after the final whistle. But tracking down players in draughty corridors for after-match interviews before facing a 300-mile return journey home on a miserable Saturday night can be interesting to say the least – especially when confronted by over-enthusiastic club officials. Asking a player for his reactions to a resounding defeat or a costly miss often takes a brave face, but to be fair Peter Reid never shirks his responsibilities even if at times he would prefer to run a mile rather than face a barrage of mundane questions.

Football is a game of opinion and the reaction of the local media to where Sunderland go from here is quite fascinating. Ian Murtagh of the *Newcastle Chronicle* has missed just two matches (one for the birth of his son James and another to attend a wedding) since joining the Sunderland beat six years ago and has been an ever-present for the last four years. He is well qualified therefore to assess the club's fortunes since they were last in the top flight.

Football has changed so much in six years. When Sunderland went up in 1990 in one sense it would not have taken a lot of investment to consolidate at that time. One of the most interesting things was just before the season in the top flight I can remember reading something in the Newcastle fanzine, *The Mag*, saying 'let's face it, we have been beaten by the enemy and just look what they have to look forward to. They have got four players who could become internationals – Gary Owers, Gordon Armstrong, Gary Bennett and Marco Gabbiadini – a forward-thinking manager and their ground is not in the state our is.'

If you think at that time, albeit Sunderland went up by default, I would say before a ball kicked off that season there was optimism of a certain kind. The first three games they played brilliantly in a 3–2 defeat at Norwich City, outplaying Tottenham in a goalless draw, and beating Manchester United 2–1. Three games into that season and everybody was saying the side was burgeoning with promise. The first half of the season there was real hope so we can't get that carried away. The fact is Peter Reid has been in the Premiership and is better equipped. He is in a position no Sunderland manager has been in since the day Lawrie McMenemy was appointed in 1985 – the club needs Peter Reid more than Peter Reid needs Sunderland Football Club.

I believe there is an unknown quantity. Everybody seems to say that Martin Scott and Richard Ord will flourish in the Premiership and I wouldn't disagree with that. But unknown factors are the Craig Russells, the Michael Grays, the Michael Bridges and the Sam Aistons. One of them could turn out to be a world beater, one of them who you think won't. Much will depend on them as much as the money Peter Reid will have to spend. Just remember when people think of Liverpool, they don't really think of big-money signings. Players at Liverpool who come to mind are Fowler, McManaman and Redknapp, who did not cost a lot. Don't underestimate home-grown talent.

I think the most significant statement in the last 12 months to come out of Sunderland's boardroom is Bob Murray saying we got it wrong last time. That is a very, very encouraging statement. The directors will be scared stiff launching that new stadium on the back of failure. Ideally I would like to think the board will give him the money to finish in the top half. I am convinced he will be given the necessary resources to ensure Premiership football in 1997/98. This must be seen as the chance for the club to take off. People have got to be 50 years old to remember when Sunderland last finished in the top half of the table. Just remember, since Sunderland last finished in the top ten, clubs like Wimbledon and Watford and several more have been there. Basically Sunderland have had this awful phrase 'sleeping giant' for a very long time. But they have a manager who has proved himself in this division in the past. They probably have the best crop of youngsters for a very long time and above all it's recognised throughout football that Peter Reid has appointed one of the best backroom staffs.

Looking back on last season people were pretty confident about the fact it was going to be better bearing in mind what Sunderland fans had gone through in the last four years or so. They were going to enjoy this season whatever because failure had lowered expectations. Sunderland fans would have celebrated just getting into the play-offs. But at the signs of success, expectations get higher and not only that, standards do as well.

The only doubt I had was after the 3–0 defeat at Wolves. Previously, after beating Millwall away, I realised this side had a chance, that the coaching methods were making the players enjoy their game on the ball. There was a method in their play and they seemed to get stronger and stronger. They have been allowed to play under this manager, but let's not forget, the side did not score in five of the last six matches and that showed three things: (a) how much in a short space of time they had come to rely on Paul Stewart; (b) very few teams have gone up scoring fewer than 60 goals (not many have gone up conceding fewer); and (c) everybody knows they have got to spend.

Anybody who looks at the games against Liverpool and Manchester United and say how well they played should forget it. Look at Bolton when they went up. They were known as brilliant cup fighters – it doesn't mean a thing. This season should not be just about guaranteeing Premiership status. Let's make no bones about it, and this is a very important point, Sunderland between next May and the following August have got to find 12,000 fans. This is 12,000 extra people who have not been in the habit of regularly watching Sunderland Football Club for a decade or more. Everybody is asuming Sunderland will have a 34,000 seat stadium and eventually 40,000. That will happen with success but this season is not just about guaranteeing Premiership football will be there for the new stadium, it's guaranteeing Premiership football with a full house. This season has got to be a case of 22,000 lucky people getting in and another 12,000 to 15,000 clamouring to get in. You can't take it for granted, but they would fill it with a successful team. What you are asking is 12,000 people who have not been to Roker Park for 20 years or more, or not been at all, to be persuaded to fork out £395 like Middlesbrough have done.

Looking back on the season I could count on one hand the full-backs who I thought were better than Martin Scott, and that includes the Premiership, and I have never seen a teenager with as much all-round ability, mentally as well as footballing, as Michael Bridges. His demeanour and quick feet and sense of anticipation, i.e. being in the right place at the right time. Some of Michael Gray's displays were breathtaking. I remember the game at Charlton in the first 20 minutes where he was just skinning two or three people at a time.

Craig Russell was on fire at times. He has added a new dimension to his game. He has got broader shoulders and he now really is a power-packed player. In the past he just had pace but he has added power. Richard Ord has got such ability in his feet after so long of the ball being like a hot potato. There are now situations where the ball is glued to his feet, and he danced out of situations.

'The biggest compliment I can pay Shay Given is, sadly, it was inevitable that Blackburn Rovers wanted him back. Paul Bracewell must be the most influential player, there is no doubt about that. If things were not going well away from home the young heads would look to him and see him there. He's been there and done it and it was not so much inspiration as reassurance.

Frank Johnson (*Northern Echo*): I thought they would do well on the strength of what I had seen when Peter Reid took over for the last seven games of the previous season. I expected Peter Reid to spark them a bit and the best I expected, because I knew he did not have very much money, was a play-off position. If they finished fifth or six, they would have done well, but I was astonished they did so well. I am pleased they did well but I think it should still be tempered, but I honestly did not think the First Division was as strong as it has been. There were a lot of teams very similar in strength and Sunderland's forte was that Peter Reid got them organised and that made the difference.

'Signing Shay Given on loan from Blackburn Rovers was a masterstoke, but at the same time Alec Chamberlain did not perform too badly and deserves credit. But while Given sort of inspired them, the player who sticks out in my mind was Richard Ord. He was the king-pin of the success. He has been at the club for ten years, which is astonishing. He is only 26 and has played all over the place out of position but his true position is central defence and he looks superb.

I was delighted to see Craig Russell come through. Playing up front is a hard position for a young local lad. They take a lot of criticism. Sunderland have tried to buy centre forwards all through their history. Bobby Gurney came out tops but he is one of the few who cost the club nothing and I hope the same could happen to Craig Russell and young Michael Gray. He did well and with a bit more maturity, he could become a good player.

I was delighted with Martin Scott. They were the outstanding talents which came through and Peter Reid got the best out of them. The others all chipped in but he gave them this self-belief. It was virtually the same team which finished the previous season – that team was a shambles. They did not believe in themselves but somehow Peter Reid got this over to them and told them they could be as good as anything in this division. They started believing and got a few breaks as well which they didn't in previous years. People say your name is on the Cup and the longer the season went on, the more belief they had and other teams became a bit apprehensive of them. Sunderland were on a roll and in the end won the First Division Championship comfortably. For me, before Dave Bassett took over at Crystal Palace, only two teams were in at Christmas – forget Millwall because they were eventually relegated. Sunderland and Derby County were the only two and Peter Reid's side was a bit unlucky to lose a ding-dong match at the Baseball Ground.

But what really convinced me Sunderland were going to do it was when they annihilated Derby at home. They just steam-rolled over Jim Smith's side. The self-belief was there; they had their hands on the trophy then. It looked as though they meant business.

I am delighted for the fans particularly. They have had so much to put up with with the success of Newcastle United up the road over the last few years.

Some of the greatest disappointments come after success. Everybody thought when Sunderland were promoted for the very first time under Alan Brown in 1964 after beating so many good teams that better times were ahead, but it was such an anti-climax. They did not start climbing; quite the opposite, they struggled. In 1973, after Bob Stokoe's side won the FA Cup, everybody thought that was the start of something big. But it was another couple of years before they got promoted and when they did go up, they came straight back down again. The same thing happened in 1990 and it would be a tragedy if the same thing happened this time round. They have a manager who obviously knows what he is doing and the board must support him in the transfer market. To go back down again immediately just before the move to the new stadium would be a nightmare scenario. That would be the blackest day in the club's history.

I was covering Sunderland home games in 1958 when they went down for the first time. I know what effect it had on the people of the town. It used to have it on the programme, the only team never to have played outside the First Division. Sunderland were a big name – it was as though somebody had died – the death of Wearside. I would consider a similar type of disaster to that if they went down again. It's up to the board to make sure the club stays up. The move into the new stadium will generate the cash to give the club the chance to be great again. Sunderland were a top-six club in the 1930s and ranked among the best in the world. Those days have long gone but I just hope the directors have the ambition and Bob Murray realises he must be the leader. He has got to strengthen the team but at the same time hang on to the young players. It would be great to see Richard Ord, Michael Gray and Craig Russell establish themselves in a good team – let them play with flair. They have had some bad times and this must be the happiest time of Richard Ord's life. He has another six to eight years left in the top flight and I hope he enjoys himself there. I don't think he will become another Charlie Hurley, but he could make a name for himself.

I would like to see a Sunderland where players can make a name for themselves again here and not have to leave like Colin Todd, Colin Suggett, Denis Tueart and Dave Watson did. It's a long time since anybody came to Sunderland to make their name – Charley Hurley was possibly the last one – and if he had been born in England he would have played for England. I would like to see Sunderland the type of club where players don't learn their trade then leave for greater things. Sunderland have the support and soon will have a stadium to match that. This should be a place where people will give their right arm to play.

I have watched them for a very long time and I would love them to have a top team. I keep telling people Sunderland were bigger than Liverpool and Manchester United and it's in living memory, not the last century. When Sunderland won the Championship three years out of four they had a hell of a team, like they did in the 1930s; then just after the war they had the Bank of England team.

People have seen what's happened at Newcastle and Sunderland can be as big as that. The potential is there and I can remember from my days covering Newcastle, they struggled on gates of 8,000. It hasn't all been a bed of roses at St James's Park.

'I would like Sunderland supporters to be able to hold their heads up high again and walk about proudly. It's lovely to see people in red-and-white shirts in the summer even though the football is finished. I want to see them justify that support – it's there, but it's now or never and if they make a mess of it this time the consequences are unthinkable.

But let's think positive. Let's go into the new stadium heads held high. We are a Premiership side and we are going to have the Premiership flag flying over the stadium in the not-too-distant future. If we go into the new stadium with our tails between our legs, it will take some digging out. It will be digging out like the miners dug coal out before them.

Tim Taylor (*The Newcastle Journal*): Tipping Sunderland for third place was a bit of bravado on my part. I fancied them to finish third.

It was just a gut feeling and anybody who knows me and the size of my gut, that is some feeling! But apart from the bravado aspect of it, I just had a sneaking feeling the man in charge was the right man, purely because he was the horse for the course.

I think it is fair to say Peter Reid is a pretty hard man. He is no softie. The feeling I had about him was that it was an extremely hard job because of all the problems going back over the years. People keep calling Sunderland a big club but you've got to go back half a century to substantiate that claim. They've had the odd moment of cup glory but have never been a consistent force in the top flight. There's been all the problems with the financial situation and it was such a hard job, I feel it took a really hard man to cope with it. Peter Reid got on with the job. He did not make any rash statements, he just cracked on with it. He is such a steeped football man and the only thing he is interested in is results and level of performances. He is very single-minded and I don't think he could care less what is written about him unless it is something which affects the club. We have all felt the flak when we have written or said something he did not like.

But I did not expect him to win automatic promotion. I went for Wolves and Crystal Palace with Charlton, Southend and Grimsby to be relegated, so you can't win them all. I think the backroom team he's got behind him are similar to him. They've all got different personalities on the outward side with Paul Bracewell the quiet guy, Bobby Saxton the extrovert, the cheerful Pop Robson and only youth team coach Ricky Sbragia surviving the cut from the previous regime.

Peter Reid is a man of the people. I think he is very much a working-class lad from Liverpool and it will have hurt him to show people the door because he is quite genuine and he won't have wanted to see a bloke out of work. But behind that he is such a hard lad, he had to get the job done right. He knew from the start he wanted the job doing his way. All the people around him have got different personalities and though most of them are bubbly, they have got a hard streak in them.

Peter Reid deals with the players in a completely different way to the press. We see the hard side of him, but the training pitch is where he comes into his own. No two ways about it, he has a real true love of football and inspires his players. When you start talking about football, he comes to life. He never criticises his players in public and is very protective. It certainly works for him.

But it's going to be interesting from now on. It was a poorish division and while they played well against Liverpool and Manchester United in the cups, they were one-offs. The hard part starts now, and while he has an awfully difficult job, who is to say we all can't be proved wrong? They had a bit of luck at the start of the winning run last season. Against Ipswich they were absolutely pulverised for the first 20 minutes and went on to win it and in the next game against Luton their centre-half was out and the right-back switched into the middle and headed a cracking own goal. That was the start of the winning of nine successive matches and sparked off promotion. An old sports editor of mine once said you make your own luck and I think Peter Reid did make his own luck. That was one hell of a slice of luck as they had won only one of the previous nine in the League. It was a turning point which everybody has conveniently forgotten, myself included. But the overriding thing was the phenomenal spirit among the players. Journalists are used to hearing the odd bit of murmuring and discontent, but I can put my hand on my heart and say that, throughout the whole season, Peter Reid never talked ill of his players and not one so much as muttered a word against him.

I broke a story about the one player who asked for a transfer and even when he submitted the written request, neither Phil Gray or his agent had a bad word to say about Peter Reid. Nobody was more critical about the lack of transfer market resources than me. I made myself very unpopular with the board for having a go for not spending, but at the end of the day Bob Murray was proved right. So far so good, he got them up without spending. Another factor not mentioned enough was Peter Reid got them up on absolutely nothing. He only had slightly in excess of £1 million and nearly all of that was swallowed up on David Kelly. Kevin Keegan and Bryan Robson before him were looking at the best part of three to four million pounds each to get Newcastle and Middlesbrough out of the division respectively. That is why Peter Reid was named Manager of the Year. The people who made the award said they always take into account how much money is spent and it was a big factor this year.

For me, though, Alex Ferguson was Manager of the Year. Anybody who gets rid of Mark Hughes, Paul Ince and Andrei Kanchelskis and wins the double has to win it. I think they are just making the trophy go round – and that's not knocking Peter Reid for one minute. It's a rare combination that a man who is so hard talking has so much enthusiasm for the game his hardness disappears when he is dealing with football. He comes to life and in that respect he reminds me more than anybody else of the late Bill Shankly. I think he models himself on Bill. He was a Liverpool fan as a kid and I think he is the new Shankly. He has those same cryptic one-liners Shanks had and the same hardness. He would have worshipped on the shrine of Shanks when a lad and, as they say when you go to primary school, that's where influences are made.

Most influential player? Paul Bracewell. 'One thing I am proud of was right at the start of the season, before a ball was kicked, I picked up on Michael Gray and predicted he could have a good season. The most startling progress was made by Richard Ord and Michael Gray, but if either had suffered long-term injuries, they may still have won promotion. But if Paul Bracewell had been out much longer they might have struggled as I consider Brace the most influential player of the season. There was a bit of luck there, too, when he decided to have the groin operation. They were not in a position to mess about – he had to have the op at Christmas time, but three games were postponed while he was on the mend and while it was a financial disaster at the ticket office, it certainly helped the promotion cause.

John Cairns (Newcastle Radio): There was a lack of self-belief in the players when Peter Reid arrived at the club with seven games to go of the 1994/95 season and most people were thinking they are never going to get out of this rut. But he came in, gave the side a bit of stability, tightened things up and there was a lot of admiration for the work he did. I think the players thought they could not give Mick Buxton any more and I think he thought the same way.

There was a grave danger the club would have been relegated and the change had to be made when it was even though Mick Buxton had indicated he would possibly leave at the end of the season. Staying up was very important but after a first-day defeat by Leicester City I did not think the side would win promotion. While it was still early days, the Coca-Cola Cup-tie at home to Preston was a turning point. Lee

Howey turned it round with two goals, obviously with the help of the rest of the team, but I think that's when they realised you can get out of jail sometimes like that.

They played some terrific football – no doubt about that – and some of the one-touch play was exceptional to watch. The players gained in confidence and Shay Given came in to play a big part. I can remember the day he arrived for training at the Charley Hurley Centre and I asked Peter Reid if anything was happening. He said he had brought in a goalkeeper on loan from Blackburn and I did not know who he was, but what an inspired loan deal that proved to be, with every respect to Alec Chamberlain.

The unbeaten run just went on and on and I felt a little bit sorry for Alec. But he came up trumps at the end of the season to play his part like so many others. I thought the signing of David Kelly would spark off a leap up the table but unfortunately he was injured shortly after he came to the club. Perhaps expectations were too high towards the end of the season when supporters thought they would just run away with the Championship. It became a case of Peter Reid instilling in his players if we don't lose this game we will be okay. It was not a negative approach. It was a case of conserving what you have – a horses for courses approach. He set his stall out in a professional manner that if you don't concede a goal, you don't get beat. It was as simple as that.

A lot of the praise should also go to Bobby Saxton. He is a quiet man – I knew him from his days with Jim Smith at Newcastle – and he gets on with the job and the players were quick to praise him for the part he played.

When you look at the youngsters like Michael Gray and Craig Russell and Michael Bridges at the tail end of the season, the future of the club is in good hands. Martin Smith did not figure too much because of injury, but I am confident he will have a big part to play in the Premiership next season. Richard Ord had an outstanding season. He was unbelievable and for me the highlight of the year. A lot of people are talking, and I am as guilty as anybody, about how much money Peter Reid will have to spend on this player and that. But when you are playing at a higher level, players raise their game and talk is of how they will fare against the Manchester Uniteds, the Liverpools and Newcastle Uniteds. All people have to look at is the

Cup games against Liverpool and Manchester United – I think that answers a lot of questions.

The players have the ability to raise their game and I believe that is going to be crucial next season. They have a solid base to build on but need a self-belief of their ability to compete at the highest level. That will be instilled by the coaching staff, but they must believe it themselves. They must go into the Premiership in the last season at Roker Park with a bit of optimism. The most important thing is to consolidate themselves and not be dragged into a situation where they are having to chase games early on in the season because they are frightened that relegation trap door is looming. The Premier League is one hell of a platform upon which to move into the new stadium come the start of the 1997/98 season. I am quite sure they will be there and it will be a great boost not only to Sunderland Football Club, but the whole of Wearside.

Charles Harrison has been the voice of sport for Metro Radio for nearly a quarter of a century, and he considers the current management team the best at Sunderland during his stay in the north-east.

Without any doubt this is the best backroom staff in my 23 years covering Sunderland. I believe there is enough intelligence there to do everything possible to keep the club in the Premiership.

Most sides promoted to the Premiership have not been as defensively sound as Sunderland and I think that will hold them in good stead. But it's fair to say they failed to score in five of their last six games and if you are not going to score goals against First Division sides, you are going to struggle against Premiership teams.

Peter Reid won't be given the sort of money Ron Atkinson had last season. He spent £14 million but Coventry City only escaped relegation on the last day of the season. But he is a much better manager than Ron Atkinson and many more in the Premiership even if I didn't agree with his Manager of the Year award. I have always been in favour of managers other than the Championship winner of the respective leagues being considered for those awards, and any other season Peter Reid would have deserved it. But Alex Ferguson deserved it. Any manager who loses three players before the start of the season then goes on to win the double should win the award.

I thought Sunderland were about fifth or sixth favourites to win the First Division and at best reach the play-offs. Derby County and Wolves were probably the best bet with Sunderland in the top half for most of the season. Even after the 3–0 defeat at Ipswich I thought they had the makings of a pretty good side. The two games with Ipswich were incredible really, the return at Roker Park a complete reversal where the visitors deserved to win. I really thought they had a good chance after watching the FA Cup-tie at Old Trafford. It came as absolutely no surprise when Steve Agnew equalised and not too much of a surprise when Craig Russell put them in front.

I had mixed feelings about the arrival of Shay Given because I thought Alec Chamberlain had done well enough. But I would now rate Given as one of the top three goalkeepers in the country.

Once they went on that winning run and beat Derby County 3–0 to get within range of the leaders, they never really looked back. They went top after winning the next match at Oldham, the seventh on the trot, and became a very difficult side to beat.

The end of season was a bit of an anti-climax. I had Kevin Ball in the studio on the Saturday afternoon they clinched promotion without kicking a ball. Kevin was being very superstitious as the commentator at the Wolves v. Crystal Palace match had not picked up the significance of Derby County's 1–1 draw with Birmingham City. Virtually everybody had given Derby three points and when they were ahead it looked as though Sunderland would need at least a point the following day against Stoke City. But Birmingham equalised and Sunderland could not be overtaken for one of the two automatic promotion places.

I had been positive, though, after they had won at Barnsley that they would be promoted. They had to battle to win that one, playing all the second-half with ten men, and they just coasted to promotion after that.

I'm very optimistic for the future. Michael Bridges and Sam Aiston are two very exciting young players who I believe will go on to become very good footballers.

Bill Mantle (Sun City Radio): I would say the same as most Sunderland supporters that at the start of the season no way would I envisage the end of season. People kept saying to me to come off the fence and say something positive. I said in the short time I have been covering Sunderland (nine years) I have seen things about to happen and it's fallen the other way for all the great runs that were going on. Last season several important goals changed games, starting with Lee Howey's double against Preston. Kevin Ball's winner at Oldham and his goal against Huddersfield two minutes after they had scored was not only very important, but very significant. A defender headed on Steve Agnew's centre, and whereas in the past the ball would have gone into the crowd, hit the post or whatever, it came to Kevin Ball. That's how hard the team worked for things like that to happen and it's a complete reversal for Kevin Ball. Instead of stopping goals, he is trying to make them or score them himself. There's been some outstanding performances from the likes of Paul Bracewell and Richard Ord, but for me it's been a team effort.

There's not been one position where if a player was not available, the side would be weakened. It's been a squad performance throughout the season even if Paul Bracewell was so influential in the early part of the season. Before his injury he held the side together and he went through a stage where the man-of the-match award was a formality. He's been there, done it and was so vital to the side. Richard Ord had an excellent season but to be fair the back four as a unit were very solid and consistent, and at the end of the season when Paul Stewart was suspended, the goals dried up.

I'm a traditionalist when it comes to football. I believe the FA Cup should be played on a Saturday afternoon and the draw for the next round made the following Monday lunchtime, and I believe there is a gap between the top division and the rest. There is so much money at stake, I just can't see them coming straight back down.

But I think Sunderland are no better or no worse than Coventry City and Southampton and I was interested to hear what Gareth Hall and Paul Stewart had to say when I was sitting next to them in one of the last matches of the season. They said what they liked about Sunderland was the fact they didn't give the ball away and that's the one big strength they had. They lost to both Liverpool and Manchester United in the cup competitions and only lost at Anfield to two great goals. That's where the gap is between the Premiership and the rest. A couple of seasons ago Sunderland played Aston Villa off the park and lost 4–1.

I've no doubt they will stay up next season even if it's going to take one or two additions to do it. I am a great fan of Craig Russell and think he is a throwback to the Malcolm Macdonald type of centre-forward – he would run through a brick wall. Peter Reid will not let any player rest on his laurels. He will make every one of them fight for their place but what the side has not got, and have not had for a very long time, is a Micky Quinn. He scores goals off his backside when standing in the wrong position and that's not something you can put into players.

I have a lot of time for Alec Chamberlain, but Shay Given is one of the best prospects I have seen in years. He is such a rough diamond but he is going to be some goalkeeper and if Peter Reid had been able to sign him permanently from Blackburn Rovers, I could see him being in goal for the next 20 years.

The younger players will blossom. There was one match towards the end of the season when seven of the 14 on duty had come through the youth policy with Richard Ord the captain. That's 50 per cent and you can't buy that because these lads are going to be around for years to come. I am very optimistic but at the same time I'm not saying they are going to knock doors down. When Kevin Ball was presented with the First Division Championship somebody said to me it is 50 years since that was last seen at Roker Park. The following season they won the FA Cup so you never know – stranger things have happened.

The backroom staff is excellent and I believe youth team coach Ricky Sbragia can go far in the game. Kevin Ball is an outstanding club captain and the players enjoy training under Bobby Saxton and Pop Robson. There's a lot of experience there and the manager has so many contacts in the game; that's why the most important signing was Peter Reid agreeing to a new three-year contract. The Championship was important to him.

If somebody had said to me before the start of the season Sunderland would win the First Division Championship and supporters would be forging tickets to get into Roker Park, I would not have believed them.

Graeme Anderson (*Sunderland Echo*): My first season as a sports reporter for the *Echo* may have seen Sunderland promoted to the Premier League, but I'll not claim all the credit! Sunderland's management team, the players and the fans deserved every ounce of praise that was heaped upon them in a fairytale season.

Personally it would be difficult to imagine a more exciting baptism into the world of sports journalism than being involved in the coverage of such a remarkable success story. And for me, as a Sunderland supporter, few things could have been more satisfying. After ten years as a hard-news journalist, I transferred to the Echo sports desk for the 1995/96 campaign and a season where few Roker fans expected exciting times ahead. There's always hope though . . .

A time-worn tradition I was rapidly introduced to on the sports desk was that article where, at the beginning of the season, journalists make predictions about who will go up and who will go down. As far as I know only one other reporter in the north-east gave Sunderland any chance of promotion. I reckoned they might fill the final play-off slot although my opinion was influenced more by defiant sentimentality rather than hard-headed objectivity.

The fact that many at the time laughed at the hopeless optimism of my prediction shows just how low expectations were of Sunderland. No one could have anticipated at the beginning of the 1995/96 campaign the sort of astonishing revival in Roker fortunes which would see Sunderland emerge as Division One champions and Peter Reid crowned Manager of the Year.

Generally speaking, Sunderland fans have two barometers for measuring success. The first is the fairly obvious: 'Where are we in the League?' The second, and even more important to many Roker fans, is: 'Where are we in the League in comparison to Newcastle?' Going by the second measurement, Sunderland have had possibly the worst spell in their history. The fans suffered agonies; their team too often in recent seasons looked utterly mediocre, struggling to make any impact, while Newcastle soared ever higher. Keegan and his charisma, Newcastle and their team of entertainers, Tyneside and its Toon Army captured all the headlines while Sunderland first under Terry Butcher and then Mick Buxton, seemed destined to sink without trace.

Last season Sunderland managed to escape relegation from the first division by the skin of their teeth; Newcastle finished sixth in the premier league after a season of rich promise petered out. On Tyneside and on Wearside the fans spent the close season watching and waiting. Keegan bought Les Ferdinand for £6 million and Warren Barton for £4 million, Sunderland bought Paul Bracewell for a price which later emerged as £50,000, and for many Sunderland supporters the writing was on the wall. The agony would go on.

Early-season form gave little indication of the Reid Revolution. Sunderland made a steady start while Newcastle got off to a stormer. But as the season wore on Sunderland rose further and further up the table turning in brilliant home performances against strong teams like Wolves, Millwall and Derby. Gradually the Sunderland fans became more and more interested in what their own team was doing and less obsessed with the efforts of their rivals up the road. Truly, as they say, it's a funny old game football – by the end of the season the envy had turned almost full-circle.

There was no doubting that Sunderland had enjoyed the most satisfying season. Newcastle fans would probably have happily settled for the runners-up spot and a place in Europe at the beginning of the campaign. But after leading at one stage by 12 points and lapping up all the hype their overwhelming feeling at the end of the season was one of disappointment. Sunderland on the other hand were left to contemplate a season where not only had they won promotion as champions but had regained their pride in convincing fashion.

The emergence of Shay Given, Richard Ord, Michael Gray, Michael Bridges and Craig Russell had given the fans heroes to cheer on. And in the 'Cheer Up Peter Reid' song they had put smiles on the faces of rival supporters across the land and done wonders for the club's public image. I do not compare Sunderland and Newcastle's fortunes out of narrow-minded parochialism. But it is important to illustrate the fact that both sets of supporters are motivated to a huge extent by pride in their club and pride in its performance next to its closest rivals. That pride on Sunderland's part had been massively damaged in recent seasons. Even adult Sunderland fans were beginning to feel ashamed of the club they supported, while for children it was worse.

It is for this reason that I believe this season was one of the most crucial in the history of the club – Sunderland's last, best chance to prove they were potentially one of the biggest clubs in the country. If the fans did not flock back as the Roker bandwagon gathered steam it was simply because the supporters had been down for so long. One more season of Sunderland shoddiness compared to Newcastle's brilliance would have spelled the end of the Rokermen as a 'big' club. Already the vast majority of 1990s kids in the region have been drawn to supporting Keegan's Newcastle. Over the last year Sunderland started to win them back. But if Sunderland had done nothing in the 1995/96 season then I believe the decline might have become terminal – it was that close. Sunderland Football Club would of course have survived but it would have been in the shadow of Newcastle and even Middlesbrough for years to come. In the eyes of the north-east's young fans Newcastle and Middlesbrough would have been established Premier League sides while they would have seen Sunderland as forever First Division and second-rate.

If Peter Reid achieves nothing else in football, then this season will serve as proof positive of his talents as a manager. He spent most of the season desperate for cash to match the money being spent by his rivals. But he never allowed himself the luxury of becoming disillusioned. He and his management team buckled down and extracted every ounce of effort and skill from a team who were never short of ability – just the right sort of management to make the most of their talents. It took time to come together.

There was little evidence of the team's potential on the pre-season tour of Ireland and early League results seemed to suggest that Sunderland would again be a team that flattered to deceive. But gradually the passing game came together, the panic when things weren't going for the side began to disappear and the sheer determination to work hard and win shone through.

There were several turning points in the season – the earliest being the second leg of the Preston North End Cup-tie. The first-half was as dire as anything I've seen from Sunderland in recent seasons, but urged on by a blood-and-thunder team talk by Peter Reid at half-time, they came back to grind out a victory. That same determination was in evidence midway through the season against Portsmouth at Fratton Park where Sunderland ground out a point in injury-time. That result saw them embark on a tremendous unbeaten run which thrilled the fans and had them fair skipping along to Roker Park. And it was that never-say-die attitude and resolve to stick to their system which was the key to their promotion.

Personally, I enjoyed several high points to my season. Of course there was the marvellous 6–0 victory over Millwall where Craig Russell and Martin Smith were outstanding. But there were also those home victories over Wolves and Derby where Sunderland dominated completely and demonstrated a level of passing play that was often breathtaking. Another moment that stands out was the sense of amazement as Craig Russell scored the second goal to lead Manchester United 2–1 at Old Trafford in the FA Cup on a truly memorable day. Off the pitch I have enjoyed seeing the fans smile again, enjoyed joining in their discussions and enjoyed getting involved with the creators of the 'Cheer Up Peter Reid' song which proved such a success.

I've cut my football reporting teeth on the youths this season and the reserves and one of the things which has given me greatest satisfaction has been watching young footballers who were playing in front of one man and his dog at the beginning of the season suddenly thrust into the limelight months later. For that reason, highlights for me were the debuts of Sam Aiston and Michael Bridges, and Bridges' goals. Other talents like central defender Darren Holloway and striker David Mawson are still waiting in the wings.

'This season Peter Reid and Paul Bracewell gave Sunderland back their pride. And even if Sunderland went straight back down again under the fiercely competitive crush of the Premier League there are many supporters who will have enjoyed the ride, thankful to have enjoyed at least promotion and one season in the top flight. But I think there is a new sense of desire about Sunderland throughout the club, from the fans to the management and into the boardroom. If Sunderland can tie down their management team and provide them with just a few million pounds I can see the club surviving and eventually thriving in the top flight. Priorities are a Premier League goalkeeper, an out-and-out right-winger, a creative midfielder and a top-quality striker who can score goals *and* bring on the club's young strikers.

An exciting season lies ahead for everyone connected with the club for new blood is most certainly on the way. Peter Reid has kept his promotion-winning team together and the months ahead will be a time of reckoning for every footballer at the club who enjoyed an unforgettable Division One season. Some will blossom, others will struggle, but that's the challenge in front of them. Sunderland got back their pride this season and I believe that by the end of next season they will have rediscovered their self-belief. That's my prediction anyway.

Most influential player?: Sunderland's championship-winning season was truly a triumph for team effort. Every player played a part and Martin Scott and Richard Ord were absolutely tremendous in defence. But the one thing the side lacked was an obvious match-winner in the style of, say, a Cantona or a Shearer. The nearest they came was perhaps in the guise of a Michael Gray or a Craig Russell.

Ironically the one footballer who could be described as a match-winner wasn't even a Sunderland player. On-loan keeper Shay Given shone out as a prodigious talent, a player who kept Sunderland in the match game after game. And in matches like that against Ipswich at Roker Park, where Sunderland should have lost by an avalanche, it was Given who made the difference between victory and defeat.

My key player of the season, though, has to be Paul Bracewell. His coolness in midfield, comfortableness in possession and ability to win the ball made all the difference to the team in so many games. Peter Reid said at the beginning of the season that the most consistent side would win the League and Bracewell was Mr Consistency. He was able to convert Reid's philosophy into action on the pitch and made it clear to the players the sort of system and style of play the management were seeking to introduce. Whenever Bracewell played Sunderland passed the ball around well and his presence seemed to reassure and calm the players around him. The below-par games he had could be counted on one hand and were usually the result of injury.

Many feared that injury to him would wreck Sunderland's season, but by the time he had to make an enforced absence because of a groin injury his job was already half done – the players understood the pattern they were expected to play and were able to maintain his playing principles. Bracewell is renowned as ultra-professional and that professionalism rubbed off and inspired the players around him who became more focused on the task in hand. At 32 years of age and with more operations behind him than the SAS, some fans had written him off before the season began. But he'll be back playing Premiership football again next season and being just as influential for Sunderland in the top flight.'

Gordon Sharrock (*Bolton Evening News*): I've known Peter Reid since he was a promising youngster at Bolton Wanderers and have always considered him to be a winner. He was a winner as a player and he will be a big winner somewhere in his managerial career, if it's not with Sunderland.

I remember him coming through the ranks with an influx of young players but he was the one who stood out and was always going to make it. He suffered a terrible knee injury when colliding with Everton goalkeeper George Wood and the game was abandoned at half-time because of the conditions. He made his comeback at Sunderland and not even another bad injury could deter him. He is that type of person. He was never given a fair crack at Manchester City after finishing fifth twice and ninth. It was a big surprise to me when they sacked him, but Sunderland's gain. He is such a good motivator and organiser and very single-minded; there is no way I can see him failing.

Ian Greaves played a big part in shaping his future. He was his mentor and he thinks the world of him. Ian Greaves was so loyal to Bolton but got the sack; I think Peter Reid thought, 'What price loyalty?' He won't be looking to just consolidate in the Premiership. Bolton set their stall to finish fourth bottom and paid the price for lack of investment. They spent £7½ million on new players but the net investment was only £2.1 million as they sold Jason McAteer to Liverpool for £4½ million.

Bolton also made the mistake of having two managers. They appointed Colin Todd and Roy McFarland after Bruce Rioch left for Arsenal whereas Sunderland will have the benefit of continuity for the Premiership. But if they want to live in the Premiership, they must be prepared to play their game and back Peter Reid with hard cash.

Epilogue

Sunderland march into the Premiership with major shareholder Bob Murray confident the big time holds no fears for Peter Reid:

> Peter was a winner on the field, now he's a winner off it, and that's important. He has managed in the Premiership quite a long time for a man who is only 39 and he played all his career at that level.
>
> He was out of the game for 18 months. He should not have been out that long but obviously keeping us up last year was an achievement. You have to change things at the right time and his availability was quite amazing. I was very surprised to hear he was available, but in him we have a man of tremendous ability. The Premiership should hold no fears for him and this club could become as big as it was in the '50s and the '30s. Last season he kept us up, this season he has jacked us up and next year we are going to an all-purpose stadium at Wearmouth. It will be the best new stadium in the country. Life is exciting at the moment. It's just great.
>
> People say I have not achieved things, but I have had three promotions, one relegation and an FA Cup Final in ten years. I think that is really something.
>
> Sunderland Football Club means business and intends to make its mark in the Premier League. We are determined to compete at the highest level and will continue to make progress under the guidance

of Peter Reid. Sunderland's new stadium will be the best in the country and it will be a momentous day when Peter Reid is installed as its first manager, beginning a new and exciting era in the club's proud history.

Less than a month after the season had finished, the directors enthusiastically announced that Reid had accepted a new three-year deal, committing himself to the club until 1999. Murray commented:

> The board are absolutely delighted to have secured the services of Peter Reid until the end of 1999. This is the most important signing Sunderland Football Club could make and a tremendous one for its supporters. In keeping with the club's new-found status and the way football is going, it's ironic the club officially joined the Premiership on the same day Peter Reid signed his contract.
>
> It's a tremendous deal for Peter Reid but I am sure he is worth every penny. Peter wants a lot of things for the club. He can see where the future of the club is going, but more important is the special rapport he has with our supporters. There is a bond that has not been seen for many decades. He can become our Shankly or Clough.

Murray, however, is fully aware he must deliver or he will be hounded out of town by a lynch mob without trial. He has pledged there will be no repeat of the 1990/91 season when Denis Smith was grossly underfunded and after just one season in the top flight, the club was back among the also-rans:

> The fans will get everything they want and more. Our number one priority is the manager and we both want the best for this club. We have all got to get together: management, players, sponsors, supporters, the media.
>
> Peter will not have the income the new stadium will generate. It's a four-year strategy and being so involved at the heart of the new stadium, I am desperate Peter will be the manager when we walk out for the first game in the new stadium in 1997/98, and it's in the Premiership. Peter has played and managed in the Premiership, I have not. He will know what is required and I hope people realise

we are funding a new £15 million stadium on a £6 million turnover. The quality of the stadium has taken more cash than first estimated. There is nothing cheap about the stadium.

People knock but I am not too concerned about those people. I am an achiever in life and it's down to our ability as businessmen to deliver. We have played our last ever Football League game at Roker Park and hopefully the last ever.

If we did not have the stadium coming along I am sure Peter would not have stayed. He would have just struggled as the club has in the past. He is not here just to tread water. I am sure the stadium will be a prime consideration in his future thinking. He has put the smile a mile wide on Wearside and the fact he is so popular with the fans is brilliant news for us on the board.

The Football League has lost a great club. Sunderland was the most famous club in the League and there was no revolt from us against the management committee earlier in the season. Sunderland has never participated in anything like that.

The first steps to fund transfer activity were taken a few days before the last match of the season when the club issued a statement of a share issue aimed at raising £2.1 million. Shareholders were advised that 14,000 new shares would be offered to existing shareholders at a cost of £150 each. Bob Murray indicated that he would underwrite the Rights Issue, injecting £1,125,000 immediately, and agreed to make a further £975,000 available if the other directors failed to take up their shares: 'The additional funding will be an investment in the future of Sunderland and Peter Reid.'

To pave the way for possible additions to the squad, the manager decided upon a mini clear-out by announcing that long-serving midfield players Gordon Armstrong and Brian Atkinson and full-back John Kay would be released on a free transfer. The decision to release the trio came as no surprise as they had played virtually no part in the promotion campaign, but the wisdom of turning down offers close to £1 million from Norwich City and Southampton for Armstrong in the not-to-distant past, must be questioned.

Seven of the side out of contract – Alec Chamberlain, Dariusz Kubicki, Andy Melville, Michael Gray, Phil Gray, Lee Howey and Paul Stewart – were offered new deals. Michael Gray and Kubicki, the only two ever-presents in the Championship-winning season, quickly put pen to paper and Reid made his first breakthrough in preparing for the Premiership by splashing out £1 million to land Alex Rae from Millwall. The Scottish Under-21 international finished leading goalscorer in two successive seasons for the London club from a central midfield position.

'He is a player I have been tracking since my Manchester City days,' said Reid. 'He is an attacking midfield player who has got good feet in football terms and can get goals from the middle of the park.'

The question has been raised many times as to why Sunderland never participated in the Charity Shield in 1973.

Bob Stokoe's side had earned a pre-season showdown with Liverpool after beating Leeds United at Wembley in the FA Cup Final. And Liverpool, as First Division champions, would have enjoyed home advantage and staged the game at Anfield. But the clash of the giants never took place because of more lucrative financial rewards elsewhere. Liverpool accepted invitations to tour Germany and Japan while Sunderland opted for games in Scotland and Ireland after a prestigious international tournament in Portugal fell through.

Instead, Sunderland completed their pre-season build-up by taking on League Cup winners Tottenham Hotspur at Roker Park with their Cup-winning side. A Jimmy Neighbour 19th-minute header won the match for the visitors.

It was because of the decision of the respective clubs to shun their domestic responsibilities that the Charity Shield curtain-raiser to the new season was switched to Wembley to become an eagerly awaited money-spinning fixture to both clubs.

Ironically, Liverpool provided the opposition for the first-ever League game at Roker Park – a 1–0 victory on 10 September 1898 – and their Merseyside rivals Everton will bring down the curtain on 3 May 1997 before Sunderland enter a new era at the former Wearmouth Colliery pit site.